Tour Site Map

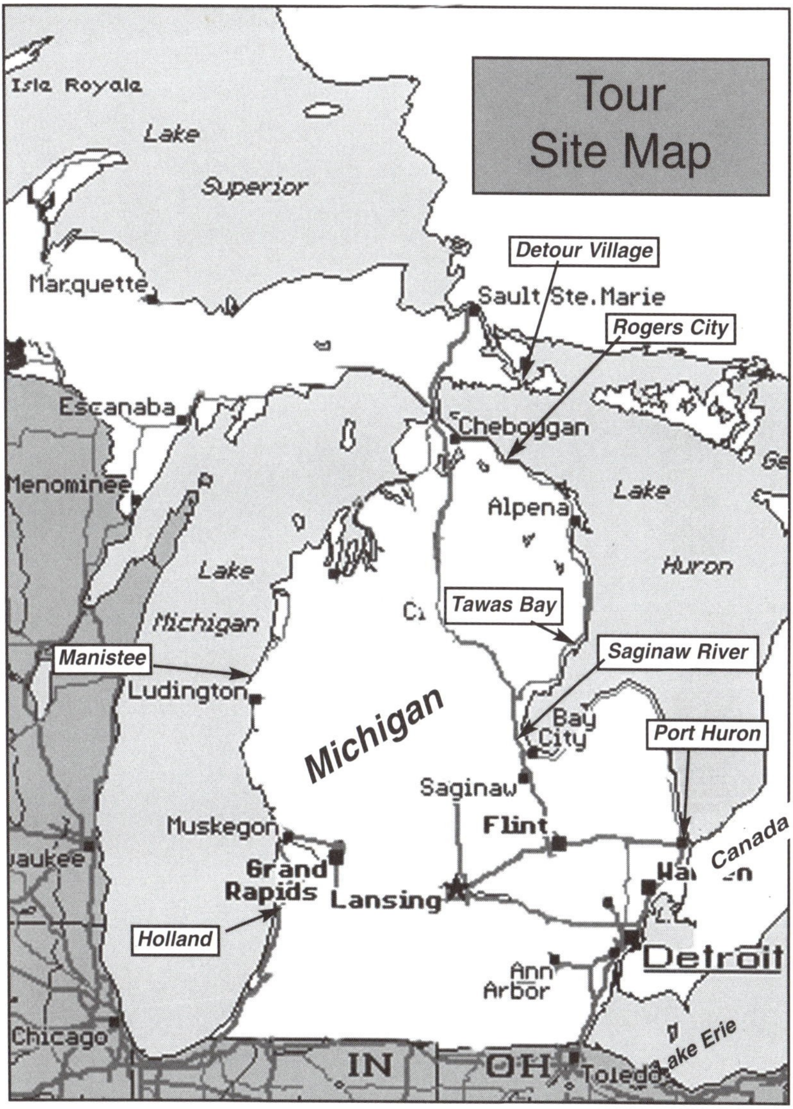

Alpena
DeTour Village
Detroit
Escanaba
Holland
Manistee
Marquette
Muskegon
Rogers City (Calcite)
Saginaw River
Sault Ste. Marie, MI (the "Soo")
Tawas Bay

A Guide To Lake Boat Watching In Michigan

(With some tips for the RV Folks)

by

Herb Hammond

A Little River Book

Copyright © 2004 by Herbert J. Hammond. All rights reserved. No part of this book may be reproduced or transmitted in any form or by any means, electronic or mechanical, including photocopying, recording or by any information storage and retrieval system, without permission in writing from the Publisher, except for brief excerpts or quotes used for reviews.

A Guide To Lake Boat Watching In Michigan by Herbert J. Hammond

Published by the Little River Books Division
J. R. Simpson & Associates, Inc.,
 2175 Huntington Dr.,
 Florissant, Missouri 63033-1227.
 Phone 314/921-4419.

First Edition

Printed in the United States of America

Library of Congress Control Number 2004111291

ISBN 0-9703086-5-5

Dedication

This book is dedicated to my wife Marguerite, and to my son, Christopher, for putting up with me.

Illustrations

Columbia Star	Front Cover
Buffalo	Back Cover
Oglebay Norton	X
Oglebay Norton	4
Edmond Fitzgerald	9
The "Cort"	16
E. M. Ford	22
Roger Blough	23
Stewart J. Cort	24
Arthur M. Anderson	26
Sykes	26
David Z	27
Edward L. Ryerson	28
John D. Leitch	29
Vancouverborg	30
Jahre Viking	32
Tanker Prestige	33
Contemporary Container Ship	34
Derbyshire	35
Stewart J. Cort	37
Presque Isle	37
James R. Barker	38
Oglebay Norton	39
Industrial Ruins at Rockport	42

Illustrations

Stoneport Activity	.43
Walter J. McCarthy	.45
James R. Barker	.50
Herbert C. Jackson	.51
"The Barker"	.52
Kaye E. Barker	.53
L. E. Block	.53
Paul R. Tregurtha	.58
"Old downtown" ore dock	.59
Paul H. Townsend	.61
Calcite	.65
Buffalo	.65
Joseph H. Frantz	.66
Wilfred Sykes	.67
Calumet	.68
McKee Sons/Invincible	.69
Canadian Transfer	.70
Columbia Star	.71
Courtney Burton	.73
Edwin H. Gott	.74
Presque Isle	.76
Sugar Island Ferry	.76
James R. Barker	.77
Kaye E. Barker	.79

Illustrations

Edwin H. Gott *80*
Buffalo *84*
Abandoned Aerial Tram *85*
Marine Diesel Engine *88*
Algowood. *89*
Reserve *90*
Paul R. Tregurtha *91*
Agawa Canyon *92*
Cedarglen *92*
Joyce L. Van Enkevort *93*

Table of Contents

Table of Contents VI

Illustrations VII

Foreword X

A Little Note on Ship Names 1

Boat Watching In General 3

Shipwrecks On The Great Lakes 8

How Are Things Going With The Lake Boat Industry? . . 14

Special Boats 21

The Mega-Ship Era 31

Alpena 41

DeTour Village 44

Detroit 46

Escanaba 52

Holland 54

Manistee 56

Marquette 58

Muskegon 61

Rogers City (Calcite) 64

Saginaw River 67

Sault Ste. Marie, MI (the "Soo") 71

Tawas Bay 83

Glossary 87

Appendix A. US and Canadian Fleets 94

Foreword

The 1000-ft. **Oglebay Norton** early on a May morning, downbound at the Soo (photo by author)

"But look! here come more crowds, pacing straight for the water and seemingly bound for a dive. Strange! Nothing will content them but the extremest limit of the land; loitering under the shady lee of yonder warehouses will not suffice. No. They must get just as nigh the water as they possibly can without falling in. And there they stand-miles of them-leagues. Inlanders all, they come from lanes and alleys streets and avenues-north, east, south and west. Yet here they all unite. Tell me, does the magnetic virtue of the needles of the compasses of all those ships attract them thither?"
Herman Melville - Moby Dick

They come every year to these places – RV campgrounds in Sault Ste. Marie, Michigan (the "Soo") – to look at the broad St Mary's' river, to fish in it, and to watch the ships pass by. Looking at the licenses on the motor homes and trailers you see a lot of folks from Michigan, but also from places in the sunbelt; Georgia, Florida, Texas, Arizona and California. Many go to the Casino in the evenings (a free shuttle stops by whenever anybody wants to go), but most settle down, light camp fires and wait. More ships will come.

And when one does, it always seems a surprise. You're sitting there, relaxed, and suddenly this huge shape silently shows in the corner of your eye. They don't make much noise - think about a diesel-powered 18-wheeler sneaking up on someone! But here is this ship – many times bigger than the truck – force-of-nature big... just gliding along enigmatically in the night.

We do really like to just watch things – all sorts of things, birds, animals, trains...and - as Melville observed – ships. The goal of some is to take pictures, but for others, just watching is enough. It is also a fact that we like to relax looking at bodies of water, and Michigan has a lot of them, including borders on all of the Great Lakes except one (Lake Ontario). For a couple of hundred years the Great Lakes have had a unique, vibrant shipping industry and that is what this book is about – where to go to see ships in the state of Michigan.

I grew up in Michigan, about fifty miles west of Detroit, but we rarely went there, so I knew nothing of the lake boat traffic on the Detroit River. My first awareness that there were such things as great ships came from watching "Victory at Sea" in the 1950's, on Sunday afternoons on a 14-inch black-and-white TV. The series of 20-some episodes was a U.S. Navy production, which essentially shows how the Navy won World War II (they never really come out and say "by ourselves", but there is a definite inference there), and the award-winning series still runs from time to time on the History Channel. My dad, who had been in the Army in the Pacific during the war, watched some of it with me. He had been on several Navy troop ships during the war, and as a result, did not have any romanticized conceptions of ships (or the U.S. Navy or Army either, for that matter) but I was fascinated anyway. What a life! Always leaving one place to go to someplace else!

The first <u>actual</u> ship I remember seeing was during a family vacation to Michigan's upper peninsula. We were in Sault Ste. Marie, MI (the "Soo") and I remember seeing a big, long ship exiting a lock and steaming away. I am sure it was a standard ore carrier, probably 500-600 feet long, but it seemed so <u>big</u>, It was so....majestic...exotic. You could say I was impressed.

After high school (Dexter, MI), I fooled around for a summer and then joined the Navy. In four years, I crossed the Pacific several times and spent time aboard various amphibious and transport ships (including two former WWII Essex-class aircraft carriers – the USS Princeton, LPH-5 and the USS Valley Forge, LPH-8, which had been converted to helicopter assault ships), and then, after a year in Vietnam, I returned to CONUS (Continental United States), got married, graduated from the "*The* University of Michigan" (it's a nice place, but they <u>do</u> sort of think a lot of themselves) in Ann Arbor, and then went to work for some 30-plus years. While my life has been good, I never lost that tugging-at-the heart of the ships.

So when we retired, we considered (briefly) Florida, Tennessee, Nevada and Savanna, GA (they have a lot of ships in and out of there), and then we moved "up north". To Michigan residents, the term "up north" is understood to refer to any location north of Saginaw. Please note that "up north" does <u>not</u> refer to Michigan's upper peninsula – although it is surely "north", it is a separate entity with it's own proud culture (they mostly root for the Green Bay Packers) and is properly referred to as the "You-Pea". When you live "up north" though, everything to the south, specifically including the Detroit area, is referred to as "down below" – "I have to go down below next week" is perfectly understood and often generates a polite commiseration.

Speaking of "local terminology"; a tip – if you want to sound like you know what you are doing around the lakes, don't refer to those ships that you are watching as "ships". They are called "boats", sometimes "lake boats", sometimes "ore boats", but never "ships". It's a Great Lakes thing, but I find myself "slipping", sometimes – it's hard for me to call a vessel that is 1,000 feet long and 105 feet wide a "boat". Some old-timers will refer to a "Salty"as a ship, but the resident Lakes fleets; U.S. and Canadian, are fleets of <u>boats</u>. Take a look at the "glossary" for some more terms.

Chapter 1

A Little Note On Ship Names

What's in a name? You won't see a lot of imagination in the names of lake boats – most are named after people – but a specific type of people, to be sure. To illustrate my point just look at the newest class built: the 1000-footers.

Ship	Named After
Presque Isle	Place (I'm not sure which one – there are lots of places by that name
Burns Harbor	Place – It's near Gary, Indiana
Mesabi Miner	Honors workers on the "Iron Range" ore mines.
Oglebay Norton	Company flagship but was originally built by Bethlehem Steel and launched as "Lewis Wilson Foy" - (Executive).
Columbia Star	"Columbia Transportation" was the name of the company when this ship was built. Company name later changed to "Oglebay Norton Marine Services". It can be confusing.
Indiana Harbor	Place - also near Gary, Indiana
Stewart J. Cort	Executive
James R. Barker	Executive
Walter J. McCarthy	Executive
George A. Stinson	Executive
Edwin H. Gott	Executive
Edgar B. Speer	Executive
Paul R. Tregurtha	Executive

2   A Guide to Lake Boat Watching in Michigan

You don't find a lot of inspirational ship names on the lakes. No "Cosmic Wanderers" or "Ocean Adventurers". Also, it is not unusual for lake boat companies to change names in mid-career; for example the Paul R Tregurtha was originally launched as the "William J. Delancy". I don't know what Mr. Delancy did to fall out of favor. Mr. Tregurtha is the current Vice Chairman of the boat's owners – Interlake Steamship. The McCarthy was originally named "Belle River" and just this year, somebody[1] renamed the Stinson "American Spirit".

It is a custom of sea-going folks to personalize ships as to gender – at least this is true with North Americans and our British cousins. Ships are always referred to in the third person as "she". It follows that quite a few ships would then in fact be named after women, and this has been true with the ocean-going fleets. Not so on the lakes. American Steamship has thirteen ships going up and down the lakes and not one is named after a woman but they do have an Adam E. Cornelius, a Sam Laud and a Walter J. McCarthy. Oglebay Norton has a David Z. Norton and an Earl W. Oglebay all right, but, again no ladies. Interlake Steamship <u>does</u> have a Lee A. Tregurtha and a Kaye E. Barker to go with the Paul R. Tregurtha and the James R. Barker and they did name a new TBA "Dorthy Ann" a couple of years ago.

Whatever the name, the traditional "she" personification is still adhered to though. Example: "I heard Big Paul (Paul R. Tregurtha) call in – <u>she's</u> upbound at Detour".

As far as the ships and boats plying the lakes go my personal, absolute favorite name is that of an ocean-going bulk carrier (which I have never seen) owned by Oceanbulk Maritime S.A., of Athens, Greece. Her name is "Strange Attractor". (Maybe it's a language thing – just doesn't translate well). I'm also fond of another Greek salty "Millenium Raptor".   But that's just me.

---

[1] The Stinson was built for and owned by National Steel, but was chartered out to lake boat companies; first to Interlake Steamship and then to her current manager, American Steamship. National was taken over by US Steel in late 2003.

Chapter 2

Boat Watching in General

Watching boats can be a rewarding aesthetic experience at its best and a harmless and relatively inexpensive way to kill time on a slow day. One thing that it isn't is, "for sure". The boat you are expecting may by very late, or not show up at all. This gets to the heart of the thing – why am I doing this? No one but you can answer that! You either feel it or you don't. If you do, the secret, and maybe the reward, is simply patience. There is no deadline...and it only matters to you.

An example – I wanted to get some pictures of one of the thousand-footers unloading at the Detroit Edison plant in St.Clair[1], MI. I planned a little – went on the internet and noted that Oglebay Norton was loading coal at Midwest Energy in Superior, WS and was scheduled into St Clair at 11:00 AM on Wednesday. Tuesday we drove our motor home to Port Huron and stayed overnight in a RV Park. Wednesday morning we crossed the Blue Water Bridge and drove south along the Canadian side of the St Clair River (There just isn't much chance of access on the U.S. side unless you own a house there and since 9-11 practically nobody can get anywhere close to a power plant anyway – besides, at 11:00 AM you would not be shooting into the sun from the west (US) bank of the river.) 11:00 came and went so I called a number (800 861- 8760) that Oglebay Norton Corp thoughtfully records every morning and learned that the Oglebay Norton, the boat, was now due St Clair at 17:00 hours (five PM).

---

[1] Actually there are two plants at St. Clair, one is called the "Belle River Plant" and the other is the "St Clair Plant". Detroit Edison owns both of them. There is only one unloading dock for coal.

4 A Guide To Lake Boat Watching In Michigan

My wife and I went to a leisurely lunch, did some shopping and basically killed time (I got nice photos of the several boats on the river and spotted the Oglebay Norton down bound – right on (corrected) time. We followed the boat down to our site opposite the power plant and watched (in awe) her angle her bow into the dock and then use the river current and her stern thruster to turn around – un-aided (no tugs) - in the channel, secure lines, elevate her unloading boom and start un-loading into the dock hopper – all in less than 15 minutes. These people are the best ship-handlers in the world! The pictures that I took were mostly worthless though, because by this time, I was facing directly west into the sun.

But it really wasn't a wasted day...it was a good day. (Until we tried to re-cross the bridge back to the U.S. – and encountered a wait at the border of almost two hours.)

Oglebay Norton crossways in the St.Clair river at the Detroit Edison plant. She is pivoting on her bow to bring the port side along the dock. Looking close, you can see the turbulence from her stern-thruster on the starboard side. Oglebay Norton is 1000 ft. long, 105 ft. wide and was originally built for Bethlehem Steel in 1978 and named the Lewis Wilson Foy. She was sold to Oglebay Norton Marine and renamed in 1990. (photo by author)

Resources and Equipment

Probably the single most helpful resource is the internet, and there is a single, indispensable site, www.boatnerd.com. Boatnerd is free and features a huge collection of pictures of all of the modern boats and an awful lot of the older ones. Maybe the single most valuable feature is called the "Information Search" which is a message board, and a very well maintained one at that. If you have a question; "Where is the Kaye Barker now?" or "What is the 'Rock Cut?', it will be answered, probably by several seasoned "nerds". The tone of the board is friendly and encourages participation - there is almost no "flaming" or profanity and the participants range from actual crew members to hobbyists, from housewives to retired Master Mariners living in Arizona. These folks are really dedicated to sharing their love of the lake boats.

Boatnerd doesn't officially track ship schedules, but there are some useful web sites that do. I was talking earlier about the western coal run – well, www.midwestenergy.com is the site for SMET (Superior Midwest Energy Terminal – owned by Detroit Edison). They post boat schedules out to several weeks. Another source on the web is www.duluthshippingnews.com, which tracks boats in and out of Duluth-Superior, Two Harbors and Silver Bay. (If you know when a boat is leaving Duluth, then you know that it will probably appear at the Soo in about 25 hours, and if it is delivering coal to the St. Clair Power Plant, then you can figure that it will appear about 19 hours after leaving the Soo. These time tables are found on BoatNerd.com.)

Another very useful tool is a VHF scanner. You can buy a scanner for less than $100 with the most useful Marine band frequencies already programmed into the devices' memory. Unfortunately, it is illegal to even have a scanner in your vehicle in the state of Michigan, regardless of whether it is turned on to a police channel or not. But you can apply, on line, for a permit with the Michigan State Police and if you haven't been convicted of any felonies recently, you stand a good chance of getting one. That might be a good thing to do, since they can lock you up and confiscate the scanner for good.

Scanners are particularly useful in high-traffic areas like the Detroit – Port Huron area channel and the Soo. In those two places, all you have to do is show up and be patient – boats <u>will</u> pass by. Follow the instructions that should come with your scanner and set it to continuously scan the marine band.

Finally, I recommend picking up a copy of the highly detailed "Michigan Atlas & Gazetteer" which is published by DeLorme (although I don't know exactly what a "gazetteer" is, it contains exceptionally detailed maps of every inch of the State). We have found it to be valuable because it includes all the little side roads that we access to get a view of boats. It is $20.00 well spent and you can find it in just about any bookstore in the state.

Favorite Sites

Boatnerd held a survey and asked folks to name their favorite place(s). A few examples:
"South end of Sugar Island"
"The LS&I dock at Marquette."
"The fantail of the Valley Camp at the Soo"
"The Muskegon channel near the USS Silversides"
"...City park in Port Huron"

and...my personal favorite,

"The front window of my apartment in Fort Worth, Texas. I don't see many boats, but it's still my favorite place, and you never know..."

Boat Watching – Notes in General

1. Look for piles of stuff. When you see big piles of (coal, salt, sand, stone, etc) near the water, it's a good bet that lake boats pulled up there and unloaded it there.

2. You can't always get there. There are some places where boats dock that you just can't get to. Power Plants, especially since 9-11, are high security locations and the public just can't get inside the gate. It's pretty cool if you own or have access to a boat, but if you don't, then you have to catch the boat coming or leaving from some vantage point that is accessible – which takes some patience. Most of the local newspapers around the lake print something about

visiting vessels. It may only be a list of boats that visited for the past week, which doesn't do you much good ("here, these are the ones that you missed last week"). But remember, they don't run these boats like an airline (for which we give thanks). They do run them very efficiently but there are a lot of variables that they are not in control of – they may have to wait to load, wait to get through the locks, be forced to slow down because of low water levels in some channel, etc.

3. If you want to get into a facility to get pictures or just get a close look at a lake boat, don't be afraid to walk up to the office or the gate shack and tell them what you want to do. More often than not, they'll let you in. Frequently, you may find that they may not let you drive a car in, but it's ok to walk. This doesn't work at some places, (I wouldn't try it at a Power Plant) but it works often enough to give it a try.

4. It goes without saying - don't trespass. Boatnerds have, in general, a pretty good reputation, and we need to keep it that way. We do not want to be known as pests. We don't want to get a bad reputation.

   Look at the Harley Davidson crowd. When I was a kid, people had a right to assume that those guys in black leather riding their hogs were very bad folks to get cross-wise of. Now days, it's pretty safe to assume that they are accountants or lawyers, but they still have that reputation to fight. Of course, a lot of people felt safer around the old-time Hell's Angels than they do with lawyers. [2]

5. Not surprisingly, 9-11 is changing things. A few companies that own docks no longer provide boat schedule information, citing Homeland Security rules.

---

[2] There, I think that's my only politically incorrect observation in this book – and I'm not even sure that it should apply.

Chapter 3

Shipwrecks on the Great Lakes

"A routine chore at sea can become a news event if Mother Nature decides to laugh at you." Fred Dutton, "Life on the Great Lakes, A Wheelsman's story"

Shipwrecks on the Great Lakes

Traveling around Michigan's coasts you will find numerous book stores and gift shops. You will typically see books on the Lighthouses as well as books about the ships. Usually, the majority of the books on ships will, more specifically, be focused on "ship wrecks". I saw one lately, titled "The 100 *Best* Ship Wrecks" (*Italics added*). The book isn't really wallowing in the macabre – it's focused on amateur divers and the title refers to the best 100 wrecks for divers to explore. It's to be expected – as humans we <u>are</u> fascinated with catastrophic events, and what is more horrendous to contemplate than a ship going down with great loss of life in a terrible storm. The Titanic comes immediately to mind (although her problem wasn't caused by a storm), but the Great Lakes has it's own famous example, immortalized by Gordon Lightfoot, in the Edmund Fitzgerald, which sank in November 1975. It is sincerely hoped that there is not great disappointment abroad in the land that nothing like the sinking of the Fitzgerald has happened on the lakes in nearly thirty years - and that it becomes less likely to be repeated all the time.

Historians and oceanographers estimate that the lakes hold the remains of thousands wrecks (estimates run as high as 10,000), and it all started out badly. The first "ship" to sail the lakes sank with all hands on her first voyage – a failed 1647 expedition to find the passage to China that French explorer Robert Cavalier was convinced existed. Cavalier (aka; "La Salle") built a 60-foot galley named the Griffin which became the first European ship to navigate the waters above Niagara Falls.

Shipwrecks on the Great Lakes 9

The **Edmond Fitzgerald** unloading cargo at Zug Island, Detroit, MI, shortly before her sinking in 1975. Built in 1958, she was 729 ft. in length and 75 ft. in the beam. She was sailed by Columbia Transportation Inc. Cleveland, OH (now Oglebay Norton Marine Transportation). This is documented to be the last photograph taken of the vessel before her demise. (photo is by permission of Mr. Paul LaMarre, Jr.)

The last total disaster on the lakes was, of course, the Fitzgerald. Some people say that the reason we haven't had others is that we just haven't had any storms like that one since. That was certainly a terrible storm, but other boats, including the Arthur M. Anderson, survived it. The Anderson was also fully loaded and had accompanied the Fitzgerald all the way across Lake Superior in the storm, and then spent several more hours looking for survivors. In fact, the final Coast Guard report of the Fitzgerald's sinking cited "...flooding of the cargo hold due to ineffective hatch closures...". More specifically "...both the crew's failure to properly maintain the hatch covers, coamings and gaskets that create a watertight seal between the covers and coamings and their failure to properly secure the hatch clamps that hold the covers securely to the coamings." Maybe it's not surprising for our era that a controversy still exists (after all, if the polls are to be believed, most people think that we don't know who shot John Kennedy down in Dallas, either).

A minority opinion holds that the Fitzgerald had actually run aground several hours earlier while passing over a shoal off Caribou Island, and that the damaged hull, coupled with the weight of the Taconite finally broke her up. The majority opinion seems to be that the Fitzgerald just broke up due to the storm. She had loaded 26,000 tons of Taconite (iron ore pellets) in Superior, WI the day before and this, in conjunction with the violent waves, just broke her back. A former crewmember was diposed by an attorney representing the crew's families and recalled "problems with her keel"and "welds breaking loose" and maybe that was it.

The last ship to be lost on the lakes was in 1979, when the Frontenaca, a 603-foot Cleveland-Cliffs ore boat ran aground in Silver Bay, MN where she was to load taconite. A sudden snow squall obscured both human and radar vision. Things might still have been OK if a buoy light had not burned out, causing the grounding. Nobody died, but the ship, after being pounded on the rocks by the storm, never sailed again and was broken up for scrap after being towed to Superior, WI.

The worst disaster on the Great Lakes resulted in over 835 deaths, but it had nothing to do with the lake's infamous storms. In 1915 the passenger steamer Eastland had boarded about 2,500 employees of Western Electric in Chicago for an afternoon excursion on Lake Michigan. While the passengers were loading, they congregated on the pier side (port), where a band was playing, causing a list towards the pier. The Ship's officers corrected this by emptying the ballast tanks on the pier side and the ship resumed level. Shortly after that, a fireboat passed on the outboard side (starboard) and the crowd rushed across the deck to that side (still ballasted), to watch the fireboat. The ship rolled over to starboard (apparently the mooring lines to the pier had been cast off) and drowned 835 people – (from Ships of the Great Lakes, James Barry"). The subsequent lawsuits were numerous and lavish.

There is no question that, contrary to intuition (after all...they are just lakes); spring and fall storms on the Great Lakes can be deadly. The lakes lie in the path of climatic battles between tropical and polar airstreams, which, when they collide, producing violent storms. The "Perfect Storm" Sebastion Unger's' description of the loss of a Gloucester, MA fishing boat, Andrea Gail, in the North Atlantic, originally formed over the Great Lakes.

"When these storms form, the water in the lakes can pile into huge waves in a relatively short time. Compared to the oceans, the smaller size of the lakes produces waves, which are typically shorter in height, but build faster and closer together. While it is extremely difficult to accurately gauge the height of waves from a ship, reports of 20 to 25 foot waves are common and estimates have ranged as high as 35 feet in some particularly severe storms". ("Steamboats and Sailors of the Great Lakes" by Mark Thompson).

So....why are disasters less likely when with "El Nino", the weather seems to be getting less predictable? Well, most of the historic incidents that resulted in damage to ships or injury to personnel weren't caused directly by storms breaking them up, as may have happened with the Fitzgerald, but by ships running into things; shoals, rocks, land or each other, in other words, navigation problems. This is not too surprising considering the numerous narrow, shallow channels that ships have to navigate on the lakes. Technology has been improving navigation steadily and continues to do so. It would be hard to argue that the professional skills of the people who crew these ships around have not improved, and that the ships themselves aren't stronger and better built than 100 years ago (for one thing, the steel used to construct ships up until the 30's was different. As was found with the case of the Titanic, the "steel" was more like "iron" and became brittle in cold temperatures, and the annual mean temperature of Lake Superior is about 39 degrees F. No disasters have occurred with the 1000-footers, or the other ships built in the seventies but there have been a few bizarre incidents:

Apparently "navigation aides" can be significant hazards themselves. Two rather extreme examples illustrate the all-too-human propensity to not pay attention to what is going on. Maybeee...they should just look out of the bridge windows from time to time?

(1) In the early (3:30 am) hours of September 9, 1993, the American Steamship's thousand-footer MV Indiana Harbor had completed some apparently routine repairs at the shipyard in Sturgeon Bay, WI and was bound for the straits of Mackinaw. All systems appeared to be working and the weather was clear when she ran into the Lansing Shoals light (approximately 10.6 miles due north of Beaver Island, and 18 miles south-east of Seul Choix Point on Michigan's upper peninsula). The Coast Guard's report concluded that; "Apparently the third mate, who was on watch, did not change course to pass through the Straits". . The Indiana Harbor struck the light house, opening a 50-square-foot hole in the bow. The crew suffered no casualties. The Coast Guard's report

12 A Guide To Lake Boat Watching In Michigan

delicately suggested that the mate "was perhaps in the wrong profession" (from "Ships of the Great Lakes", James Barry). The light house sustained $112 thousand dollars in damage, but continued to work flawlessly. The ship turned around and headed back to Sturgeon Bay for $1.9 million in repairs (where they were no doubt glad to see her again).

(2) In 1997 another state-of-the art American Steamship vessel, the MV Buffalo (634 ft, launched in 1978) encountered a problem. At mid-morning of December 12 the Buffalo was steaming downbound (beatifically, one must assume) ,in clear skies and calm water, on the lower Detroit River when she was ambushed by the Detroit River Lighthouse (which had been in the same place since the late 1880's, when it was built as a navigation aid). In spite of sophisticated radar and GPS navigation, the experienced officers and crew managed to ram the base of the light, which resulted in a "..stove in bow, like a pop can that had been jammed upon a brick" (from Lighthouse Adventures, Wes Oleszewski). There were no casualties and the Buffalo managed her way to Toledo where she was laid up for $1.2 million in repairs. The Detroit River Light survived without damage. The crew members on duty were fired, but presumably given letters of recommendation for work in the fast-food retail industry.

When things go wrong and damage results or individuals get hurt, the folks of Harbor House write about it in their "Great Lakes Seaway Log" (www.harborhouse.com). Here is a summary for the years 2000 and 2001:

10/23/00 - An integrated tug/barge, Undaunted/Pere Marquette 41, carrying 5,000 tons of pig iron from Calumet Harbor in Chicago to Marinette, WI ran into 30 mph wind gusts and eight-foot seas and cargo and equipment shifted, forcing the tug to disconnect from the barge (standard procedure in case of a problem). While disconnecting, the barge opened a 2 ft. hole in Tug forcing the tug to ground herself, The storm opened a 300 foot tear in the barge's side and the cargo was lost. No one was injured.

08/11/01 - The Canadian boat Windoc (730 ft, 1959), owned by W.N. Paterson & Sons of Thunder Bay, ON had her bridge sheared off when a Welland Canal bridge closed too soon. There were no deaths or serious injuries to the crew members. The cause of the accident was not immediately known.

10/23/01 - One of the most cherished traditions on the Lakes is that of the "Detroit Mail Boat", the 45-foot J.W.Wescott II that delivers mail (the post office designates a unique zip code for the service - 48222) and other services to ships passing through the Detroit River. Although the Wescott comes alongside thousands of ships each year she apparently swamped when she encountered rough water while delivering a pilot to a Norwegian-flagged ocean-going tanker off Zug Island. The Captain and one deckhand were killed in the incident, which remains unsolved. The Wescott was subsequently raised and is back in business delivering the mail.

But, the bottom line is still that we are talking about what has happened in the past, when we know that tomorrow ...or next week could bring another disaster. It's out there – waiting for it's time, and all sailors know it.

14 A Guide To Lake Boat Watching In Michigan

Chapter 4

How Are Things Going With the Lake Boat Industry?

"The truth was a fine thing, but it had to be its own reward" Robert Stone – A Flag for Sunrise

Well, Not good, according to the last annual report of the U.S. Lake Carriers' Association, the trade group that represents the U.S. fleet owners. The report begins; "2002 was another disappointing year..." and then goes on to cite the numbers Iron Ore shipments increased 2.7% over 2001, but the total for the year of 48.2 million net tons still represents a big 25% decrease from 1997. What was special about 1997? Well, the next year, 1998, saw a significant increase of imported steel from all over the world (but Russia and Brazil seem to get more fingers pointed at them than others). The report doesn't mince around: "...before the United States became the dumping ground for the world's excess steel making capacity." Iron ore, from which steel is made, has been the primary commodity cargo of the lake's shipping industry for well over a hundred years.

Here is the tale of the numbers for the last six calendar years:

U.S. Flag Carriers – Shipments (Millions of Net Tons)

Cargo	2003	2002	2001	2000	1999	1998
Iron Ore	42.2	48.2	46.9	60.3	57.6	63.5
Coal	21.2	21.7	21.9	20.7	21.6	22.1
Other*	4.2	4.9	5.9	5.7	6.3	6.1
Totals	91.3	101.3	96.6	107.4	107.1	113.7

* "Other" includes cement, salt, sand and grain shipments (in Millions of Net Tons)
*Author's Note: The US trade group – Lake Carrier's Association (www.lcaships.com) has not yet released the 2003 Annual Report as this book goes to press. The 2003 totals shown are thus a "rough" estimation.

These aren't the exact numbers – (see note above) and I also rounded them off. But that shouldn't interfere with the point that the Association wants to get across – the last three years have been very bad for the biggest commodity, ore, and the situation has affected boat watching. During most of 2003 at least 10 boats never came out of their winter lay-up berths. Interlake Steamship's CEO gave an interview and predicted that if the present conditions continued, the U.S. fleet would be reduced to thousand-footers only (They continue to make money.), and a few "river-boats" to service the smaller, confined ports.

But, although the above chart doesn't show it, things began to change in the last quarter of the year. 53 boats were back to work by the time the Soo Locks shut down on Jan 25, '04 and the ore shipment total for that abbreviated month was a whopping 3.5 million tons, well above any of the previous five January totals (avg: 2.2 million tons). As this is being written, things show no signs of slowing down – ore shipments tripled over the previous year for the month of March and Coal, Limestone and Aggregates are keeping pace.

The issue of how many and what kind of lake boats are viable is on the back burner for right now, although it seemed to be coming to a head as recently as early last fall when CN (Canadian National Railway) announced that it had reached agreement to purchase Great Lakes Transportation, which owns the eight boats which are descended from the old US Steel fleet. The total package that CN acquired, in addition to the boats, included two critical stretches of railroad in Minnesota and Ohio-Pennsylvania, the Duluth, Mesabi and Iron Range ore docks in Duluth and Two Harbors plus other facilities on Lake Erie. CN indicated that the boats would be operated by Keystone Great Lakes Co, of Bala Cynwyd, PA to comply with the Jones Act (which says that cargo carried between two U.S. ports must be carried by U.S. flagged ships). In reality, nobody knew what the future held for the remaining descendents of the once mighty "Pittsburgh Fleet". CN is a railroad company – and railroad companies have wanted the ore and western coal business for years now. There were, in short ominous signs; world scrap rates for ships are currently at historic levels.

It is not just the lake boat companies that are affected, of course. Bethlehem Steel went into Chapter 11 in late 2002 and was taken over by International Steel Group (ISG), which now also owns LTV's Steel operations. National Steel was acquired by

16 A Guide To Lake Boat Watching In Michigan

US Steel. Inland Steel was acquired by ISPAT – a South African company, in 1998. Since the foreign steel invasion in the late 90's, no fewer than 17 American steel companies have gone out of business and 17 others have been acquired, mostly by foreign companies, the latest being Rouge Steel in Detroit, which has announced that it has been acquired by a Russian steel company, Severstal. There is a real human tragedy to this. The acquiring companies seem to have one, very big, issue which is "legacy costs"[1] - they don't want to pay retired employee's health care benefits and some of the pension funds are "woefully under-funded". In March of 2003 Bethlehem notified 95,000 retired employees that their health care and life insurance benefits are "cancelled".

The "Cort" displaying her new "ISG" colors while passing Mission Point. (photo by author)

---

[1] Predictably, some look at this differently; "Specifically, legacy costs are the billions of dollars of benefits promised to retired union steelworkers. They are the legacy of greed: demands made by the United Steel Workers Union that were economically irrational, but agreed upon because management assumed it could pawn off its obligations on taxpayers. Unfortunately, that assumption may ultimately prove correct". Dan Ikenson, Cato Institute.

How Are Things Going With The Lake Boat Industry?

Most of this was not a complete surprise – it was being predicted by "forecasters" as far back as the 70's. The U.S. economy would move away from heavy manufacturing and concentrate on technology, which became the "information age". According to the gurus, things like steel making would move to other parts of the globe where labor costs are lower and where they couldn't afford to worry about pollution. The gurus never said it would be painless.

One of the problems that our steel industry has is that you can mine iron and make steel a lot of places on this planet. We have mined ore on the Mesabi and Marquette ranges hard for over a hundred years and haven't made much of a dent in the supply. Most of the ore is still there. Our labor and overhead costs make it difficult though.

The Bush Administration responded with tariffs[2] in 2002 and the Lake Carriers report applauded that action, noting that steel prices were at or near a 20-year low. But they also noted, in their 2002 Annual Report that:

"Until foreign steel makers stop turning to their governments for handouts and other supports and start the painful process of shutting down unneeded capacity, the American steel will always be at risk. No mill, no matter how efficient, can compete with foreign treasuries bent on maintaining employment at home no matter what the cost. The United States must have a strong domestic steel industry to support its economic well-being and its national defense capabilities. Until the principle of free but fair trade is engrained in the world steel market, Congress and the Administration must take steps to protect America's steel industry from predatory pricing and dumping."

That may sound a little disingenuous to some. Business leaders tend to recite mantras about the wonders of "free competition" except when they are losing, and then compeition is "unfair", "cutthroat" or "predatory". It is also true that lake boat commerce is at one end of a long chain of "derived demand". Economists and con-

---

[2] The Tariffs on foreign steel came off on December 5, 2003 following threats from the World Trade Organization. Among the retaliatory measures proposed by the WTO were stiff sanctions on Florida citrus products and North Carolina fabric products. The Bush folks backed down, stating that the Tariffs had "done their job". The "Sunbelt Strategy" won.

sultants use this term – the demand for boats to move iron ore from where it is mined to where it is made into steel is "derived", ultimately, from somebody else, somewhere, wanting to buy a car, or put up a building, and demand is historically cyclical. The last major period of hard times for the industry was in the early 1980's, and it was followed by a vigorous recovery.

But the recovery each time gets smaller, which gets back to the American steel companies. It seems that once one of the steel companies has to shut down, that's the end of it. The intensively competitive world market doesn't allow you to get back up on you feet once you've slipped. Many of the blast furnaces in the U.S. have not been maintained and companies teetering on the brink of bankruptcy can't find the money to refurbish them so once they fall, they can't get up. "...given the assumption that if one of those blast furnaces goes down it'll never start up again." (James R. Barker, Chairman, Interlake Steamship Co in a interview with American Maritime Officer magazine).

And a lot have gone down. Since 1997, 35 U.S. steel companies have filed for Chapter Elevens and, and was noted earlier, half of those are just flat out of business. Not all were in the Great Lakes region, of course, but the "forecasters" of the 70's are looking pretty good for now. The tariffs will never come back.

Throw in the fact that the US Dollar has been a significant factor in the problem and you begin get a picture of how complicated the problem is.[3] Is there any good news? There may be.

---

[3] "Overvaluation of the dollar against other currencies has negatively affected the cost position of US steel (mills) against foreign competitors. The vaunted cost competitiveness of most foreign steel producers, where it appears to exist, is based not on superior thecnological and enconmic efficiencies, but rather on the weakness of their own currencies against the overvalued US doller. Thomas A Danjczek, Steel Manufactures Association, July 2001

Mini-Mills

If there is a growth sector in the U.S. Steel Industry, it is in these, developed in the U.S. to reduce pollution, they were originally used to re-claim scrap steel. They are busy now making steel from imported "slab iron". A Mini-Mill may have everything that a traditional, so-called "integrated" steel plant has, except a blast furnace. It lacks the capacity to take in iron ore (read "Taconite") and make steel from it. The driving strategy that created Mini-Mills was based originally on exporting pollution to 3rd World countries that could afford it, apparently. Move the blast furnaces someplace else, where they have other priorities, like "feeding" their people, and where they are less environmentally driven.

But, back at the Lakes, some very smart and dedicated people may have come up something that could breath new life into the domestic ore trade. A pilot plant has been set up in Silver Bay, MN to process taconite ore into "nuggets" which are "96% iron" (traditional Taconite Pellets, the mainstay of the lakes ore trade for many years are 67% iron content). The goal of the operation is to produce ore that could be processed into steel by Mini-Mills, thus opening opportunities up to customers that couldn't be served. (Only 38 U.S. blast furnaces have survived the current crisis) This, of course, could mean new life for the lake boats. In spite of all the hard marketing that the railroads have done trying to get more of the ore and coal business, the fact remains that it takes six 100-car trains to carry what one 1000- footer can on a single trip.

Can the Lake Boat Industry survive? Not without some changes. The biggest single operating cost for a working boat is labor (Insurance costs are right up there too, of course). The older boats are more vulnerable because they carry less cargo, but require the same number of crew as the 1000-footers. Significantly, the last three "new" boats constructed have all been conversions of older ore carriers to self-unloading Articulated Tug/Barges (see glossary) chiefly because the Coast Guard regulations allow them to operate with much smaller crews.[4] It would not be surprising to see some more of the older, steam-powered boats in the Great Lakes converted.

---

[4] A standard ore carrier crew size was 33 in the early seventies, and it has been pared down to 24 for Self-unloading Diesel-powered boats. A self-unloading ATB comes under a "Tug Boat" classification and most carry a crew of around 12.

The Lake Carriers Association report does not cover everything that is going on. It does not talk about a very basic problem, which they share with the U.S. Steel industry. It's alluded to by the paragraph above and it is immutable. Apparently the reason is the Jones Act of 1920 in which Congress mandated that cargo carried between US Ports must be carried by US flagged and crewed ships.

One of the neatest vacations in the world is taking a Panama Canal cruise. I remember standing at the rail as our cruise ship was passing through the Gatun Locks on the Atlantic end of the Canal, when a lady standing next to me exclaimed "Why aren't there any American ships?" I realized that she was right. None of the big container ships that we had passed flew the US flag on their stern and most of them were registered in Panama, Malta, Liberia – anywhere except San Francisco or Baltimore. Where is the US merchant ship fleet? Do we even have one anymore?

The answer is; <u>Americans</u> do own a lot of ships, maybe a majority of the ships we saw were ultimately owned by US companies or individuals, but they own them through offshore holding companies (they can be referred to as "tax shelters"), they register them in other countries ("Flags of Convenience") and they crew them with people from practically anywhere <u>but</u> the US. This is not illegal or sinister; it's simply a matter of economics.

There <u>will</u> be boats to watch for a long time. The majority of them right now are Canadian owned and operated[5], but there will be boats out there hauling stuff around the lakes for as long as they can pay their way. And, to answer a big question alluded to at the beginning of this section; Why is the lake boat trade suddenly booming? The "easy" answer would be that world prices for "steel" have risen, making it feasible to add some folks to the night shift and crank up a few blast furnaces. Why did prices rise? The US dollar has dropped a little relative to other world currencies. How long will it last? Nobody knows.

---

[5] Canadians may own them, but they will have to set up US subsidiary companies to operate them. Only US owned and operated vessels can carry cargo between US ports as a result of the "Jones Act" legislated into law by Congress. This is a significant issue that does not make the nightly news, but is a bitter point of contention between the two countries.

Chapter 5

Special Boats

Special Boats

I call these "special" because, in one way or another, each of them is. The list is subjective, I admit, but, then - it's my list. Note: they are not in any order whatsoever. (Author's Note: this list is an idea that I borrowed from J.A. Baumhofer, author of "Where The Boats Are", a great guide to boat watching in Duluth-Superior.)

Str. E. M. Ford.

The Ford is unique because she is the oldest boat in the current list of active lake boats. "Active" is used advisedly because, although she is currently performing a commercial task, she hasn't sailed since 1996. But she is easy to see – she is tied up at the LaFarge Cement dock in the Saginaw River where she is used as a storage/transfer barge.

Built in 1898, she was christened "Presque Isle" and was chartered to the Cleveland Cliffs compan, and she hauled ore for that company until the mid-fifties when she was sold to the Huron-Portland Cement company of Alpena, MI., and converted to a cement carrier, and evidently renamed.

22 *A Guide To Lake Boat Watching In Michigan*

The **E. M. Ford**, owned by Inland Lakes Management (450 ft. in length, 50 ft. beam, built in 1898). She is seen at her static berth at the Lafarge cement dock on the south side of the Saginaw River in Carollton, MI. (photo by author)

The Ford still looks to be in good shape, and just think, in addition to surviving two major wrecks (in 1956 and 1979), she has sailed under 19 US Presidents, through all of our major wars but three (Revolutionary, 1812 and Civil), and seen more storms than you want to think about. She is a living piece of history and is still contributing as she celebrated her 106th birthday in May, 2004. (Author's Note: The oldest lake boat still sailing on the lakes is almost certainly the "Southdown Challenger". She was built as a ore boat in 1906 and, like the Ford, later converted to a cement carrier.)

M/V Roger Blough

The Blough, is both a "First" and a "Last". "First" because she was the first of the "super-carriers", built to take advantage of the expanded Poe Lock. Although she is "only" 858' in length, her 105' beam pushes her into the "wide-body" class in terms of carrying capacity. "Last" because she is truly the last boat built to the traditional "fore and aft" deckhouse design. The USS Great Lakes Fleet commissioned her in 1968, to be ready when the new lock at the Soo opened in 1970, but a serious fire in her engine room occurred during construction and she did not emerge from the shipyard until 1972.

Special Boats 23

Two views of the **Roger Blough** USS Great Lakes Fleet (858 ft. in length, 105 ft. beam, 1971) shown downbound in the upper St. Marys river (above) and near Mission Point, after transiting the Poe lock. (below). The shuttle-type un-loading system can be seen in the large opening in her starboard quarter. (photos by author)

The Blough also was the first boat to be equipped with the "shuttle" type un-loading system. Instead of the traditional centerline unloading boom, she has a shuttle conveyor which can be extended to either side of her stern. Supposedly, this system is faster and more efficient than the standard system, but it limits the boat to certain ports which are equipped to handle it (The Blough was designed to carry taconite to US Steel facilities in Indiana and Conneaut, OH). In addition to the Blough, three other boats were equipped with similar unloading systems; two of them were USS Great Lakes "1000-footers"; the Edwin Gott and the Edgar Speer, although the Gott has since been converted to a conventional "boomer", and the fourth "shuttler" is the "Cort"- my next special.

M/V Stewart J. Cort

So much has been written about the Cort, that I hesitate to say much at all. She was the first "1000-footer" on the lakes and she looked like a massive version of a traditional lake boat. Well, she does have two deckhouses, although nobody lives in the aft one – it's completely taken over by her shuttle-type unloading system. The engineers live in the forward deckhouse with the rest of the crew and commute aft to the engine room by golf cart. By now, she has paid for her owner's investment a number of times over, but none of the other members of the 1000-foot club saw the need to reproduce her. Instead, an entirely different design of ships were built to staff the fleets.

The Stewart J. Cort, shown upbound at Mission Point.. Built and owned by Bethlehem Steel, She was the first 1000 footer. (1000 ft. in length, 105 ft. beam, 1972), (photo by author)

Although, (or, maybe because..) the Cort seems destined to be a "one-of-a-kind", she is a big favorite of ship-watchers who love the unique boats. If you get a chance to see her (The Soo would be the best place, since her standard run is carrying Taconite from Superior, WS to Burns Harbor, IN) be sure and note the big "#1" painted on the front of the aft deckhouse – it's there for a reason.

Str. Arthur M. Anderson

This is another traditional favorite with boat-watchers, but not because the Anderson is unique in design – in fact, she is just one of a good-sized family. Added ore-carrying capacity was needed for the Korean War, and a total of 10 ore boats that came to be called the "AAA sisters" class were constructed in 1952.

Original Name	Current Status
Arthur M. Anderson	Active – USS Great Lakes Fleet
Edward B. Green	Active – now Kaye E. Barker, Interlake SteamshipFleet
Sparrows Point	Active – now Buckeye, Oglebay Norton Fleet
Cason J. Calloway	Active – USS Great Lakes Fleet
Philip R. Clark	Active – USS Great L:ales Fleet
Elton Hoyt 2nd	Sold to Lower Lakes Towing and re-named Michipicoten
Charles L. Hutchenson	Became Ernest R. Beach and later Kinsman Independent, Retired at end of 2002 season
John G. Munson	Active USS Great Lakes Fleet
Johnstown	Sold to Ford Motor Co. and renamed William Clay Ford. Sold for scrap in 1984.
Marine Robin	Active – WWII Ocean vessel converted to lakes ore boat Joseph H. Thompson. Converted again to self-loading barge in '91 for Upper Lakes Towing.

As the chart shows, eight of the "sisters" are still active on the lakes trade. Four, including the Anderson, are still with their original owners. All, of course, have been upgraded to self-unloaders and lengthened.

The Anderson is special in the hearts of the boat fans because of her crew's courageous search for survivors following the Fitzgerald's sinking. In storm conditions that kept more prudent Captains in shelter, Capt. Bernie Cooper and his crew combed the area for hours – in vain, as it turns out, but their search is symbolic of one of the classic examples of the best that is in man – to risk everything in order to save other humans. So the Anderson is beloved because she was "there, when"!

Str. Arthur M. Anderson, USS Great Lakes Fleet, (767 ft. in length, 70 ft. in beam, 1952). Shown upbound in the St. Mary's River at the Soo. (photo by author)

Str. Wilfred Sykes

The **Sykes** shown outbound near the mouth of the Saginaw River. She is 678 ft. in length, 70 ft. in beam and was launched in 1950 for Inland Steel, and immediately assumed the title "Queen of the Lakes", as the largest carrier in the fleet. She turned 50 in 1999, and is owned and sailed by Central Marine Logistics, Highland, IN. (photo by author)

Most veteran boat watchers would agree that the Sykes is the best looking boat on the lakes (now that her younger fleetmate, the Ryerson, is laid up). She has, in the ship vernacular, "nice lines". You will also hear "If you think she's pretty now you should have seen her before they hung that damn unloader boom on her!"

(Well, if the Sykes hadn't been converted to a self-unloader in 1975, we probably wouldn't be seeing her at all. She would no doubt be laid up like the Ryerson.)

Like the Anderson, the Sykes also has a history of "going in harms way", She and her crew were cited by the Lake Carriers Association for rescuing survivors from the Str. Henry Steinbrenner which sank in Lake Superior in 1953, as well as participating in the search for survivors of the Edmund Fitzgerald.

M/V David Z Norton

"David Z" downbound at the soo after transiting the MacArthur Lock. This boat is 630 ft. in long and 68 ft. in the beam, built in 1973 as the William R. Roesch. (photo by author)

The David Z. Norton is another, very successful, transition ship. She was built under Title XI of the 1970 Merchant Marine Act and was actually the first boat on the lakes completed under that act, and the first American boat built to the "new" design standard with a single, aft deckhouse. Her length and beam make her ideal for "river boating", and she was specifically designed for "trans-shipping" ore from the terminal in Lorraine, OH to steel mills located up the Cuyahoga River in Cleveland, where the larger ships cannot go. She is also a frequent visitor to other river facilities such as the Rouge in Detroit and the Saginaw.

The David Z. was originally named the William C. Roesch and sailed for Kinsman Marine Transit until 1994 along with her identical fleetmate Earl W. Oglebay, which was originally named the Paul Thayer.

Str. Edward L. Ryerson

Ryerson shown in Sturgeon Bay, WI, where she has been laid up since 1999. Built in 1960, she is 730 ft long, 75 ft in beam and the last straight-decker built. (photo by author)

Like the Cort, this boat has had much written about her and many, many pictures taken of her. During her active career she was a big favorite due to her looks and speed. She was originally built by Inland Steel, and they obviously wanted to build something special and beautiful. But Inland was bought by ISPAT, a South African holding company, and she is now owned by a U.S. subsidiary, Central Marine Logistics. Some still think that economic conditions might change enough to make her return to hauling cargo economically feasible.

Maybe the best outcome that can be foreseen for her is retirement as a museum ship. There have been periodic "open-house" weekends with guided tours led by former crewmembers during her layup, which have drawn good crowds and that would seem to be the best we could hope for as a future for her. In the meantime, we all should be glad that somebody seems to be taking good care of this work of art.

M/V John D. Leitch

MV John D. Leitch (730 ft. long, 78 ft. wide, built in 1967.) She is shown downbound in the St.Marys river and has just passed her upbound Upper Lakes Group fleetmate, the Canadian Transport. (They both saluted, so they must be on speaking terms)

    If you were to plot a spectrum – Style vs. Functionality for lake boats, the Ryerson would probably be at one end and this boat might be at the other. There are some similarities between the two; both were built in the 60's and they are about the same size, but that's about it. The Leitch was built with a diesel power plant and a self-unloading system which was upgraded in 2000 at the same time as her holds were expanded and she now can carry more than the Ryerson (27,500 tons vs. 31,600 tons). Originally christened "Canadian Century" her name was changed along with the other updates in 2000.

    The thing that you notice first about this boat is her forward deckhouse which has been described as resembling "a small-town bank building". I can only assume that the idea was to conserve deck space. You have to congratulate her owners and builders though, because she continues to be a very successful lake boat and she, unlike the Ryerson, is still hauling stuff up and down the lakes, making money for the owners and providing jobs for people.

M/V Vancouverborg

The **Vancouverborg** alongside the Marine Terminal Dock in Duluth, MN. She is 433 ft. long, 52 ft. wide and was built in 2000 (photo by author)

Like the Anderson, this Salty is definitely not unique in design, but the Dutch, at least, still know how to build good-looking, general-cargo ships like the Vancouverborg. She is owned by Wagenborg Shipping of Delfzul. Wagenborg doesn't fool around - they have built no fewer than 33 of them, beginning in 1997. Most of the fleet is between 420' and 450' loa and 40' to 50' in the beam, requires a crew of 12, and can go anywhere with various cargos. These stylish little ships are seen fairly frequently on the Great Lakes, hauling mostly grain and other bulk food - everything from wheat to sugar beet pellets. They are fast, adaptable and...they look nice.

Chapter 6

The Mega-Ship Era (The Thousand-footers Come to the Lakes)

The 1970's ushered in the world-wide era of the super-ship. Mankind has always wanted to build things bigger; pyramids, skyscrapers, dams, shopping malls and...ships. Japan in particular was poised with modern shipyards; ready to deliver "BIG" ships to the world. And they did, and because the super-tankers, which understandably got a lot of publicity, were efficient (economical) at hauling crude oil, the industrial world has held its breath and enjoyed the lower gas prices that ensued. We hold our collective breath because at anytime a huge, clumsy ship carrying 300,000 tons of crude oil can have problems, which might take years to clean up. The mega-ships attracted the attention of environmental groups early in this period (remember that the environmental movement really got off the ground in the early 70's also) and the public was bombarded with scary scenarios. Many of the points raised were valid, because there had been spills and wrecks (184 since 1976) and some of the ships really were un-seaworthy by almost any standards. But "true believers" sooner or later, seem to feel compelled to fall prey to hubris and this was no exception.

A campaign was launched with the emphasis on "Big" (as in "Big and Scary") that tried to build fear of supertankers as being, in some way, outside of the accepted laws of nature. Mysterious "vibrations" produced by supertankers would kill off the world's endangered whales. The "Coriolis Effect", which had previously only been the occasional concern of airplane pilots was cited as a dangerous issue. The coriollis effect describes what happens when an object moves north or south with respect to the earth. The earth rotates at a constant rate, which is about 994 miles per hour (1600 km/hr) at the equator. Move north (or south) a ways and you

The biggest ship to date is the **Jahre Viking**, which is classified as something called VLCC (Very Large Crude Carrier). She is 1504 ft. long and 226 ft. in the beam. That's right – over a quarter of a mile long! (photo by intertanko.com)

find that the rotational speed is a little slower – because the diameter of the "great circle" at that latitude is smaller than at the equator. The implication is that a super tanker navigating due north (or south) must adjust for the effect caused by the bow and stern rotating around the earth at different rates – or, by implication, they will be hopelessly lost, miss Newfoundland, run aground in Greenland and cause an environment disaster. Well, it could happen if everybody aboard was sound asleep for a couple of days.

The construction of the new ships was also cast into doubt. The Far East's ship yards pioneered "modular" construction that was criticized vigorously. "The traditional way of building a ship is to do so methodically from the keel to truck on an inclined slipway down which it eventually slides into the water" (from "Super Ship", Noel Mostert). The new Japanese technique involved building "modules". The bow, stern, and as many mid-sections as are desired are built separately and then welded all together. This saved construction costs by applying production-line techniques that were more efficient than the older "artisan" methods. The so-called "erector-set" method was deemed to be inferior and dangerous although U.S. shipyards had built hundreds of Victory ships during WWII using this same basic method (some are reported to still be sailing). All of the Lake's 1000-footers were built using this technique, several with "modules" built in different shipyards, and today virtually all new ships are built in "pieces". Actually, as you may have noticed, we build a lot of residential houses in "modules" now too.

The most valid criticism of the "super-tankers" was that many of them were "single-hulled". Given the construction cost savings with a single hull, a new super tanker could pay for itself with four round-trips from the Persian Gulf to Japan or Europe. Numerous oil spills from single-hulled tankers spurred a global ban of this construction in 2001, and all existing single-hulls were to be taken out of service by 2010. But things seem to have come to a head in November of 2002 when the Prestige, a 26 year old, single-hulled, super tanker broke up off the coast of Spain carrying 70,000 tons of crude oil bound for Singapore. Cracks were detected in the ship by an American Bureau of Shipping inspection in 2001 and she was supposedly repaired in China, bringing to the fore still another problem with international shipping,

"The Prestige is Bahamas flagged, American classed, Greek owned by a company that may or may not be registered in Liberia, and chartered by a business that could be Russian or Swiss. Nobody yet knows."[1]

Tanker Prestige prior to sinking. (photo by Guardian Newspaper Ltd.)

---

[1]Press release by David Cockroft, General Secretary, International Transport Workers Federation.

There are signs that this situation could be beginning to get itself straightened out – the Norwegian owner of the Sea Giant, the second largest ship ever built (1360' long), has sold her for scrap. Maybe he knows something about her that worries him and authorities do know where he lives!

Oil tankers aren't the only type of ship affected with the upsizing boom. The world's ocean-going "general cargo" ships have thrived due to "containerization" and have also mushroomed in size, but most are restricted by the need to fit through the Panama Canal (max length: 294.1 m = 964.8 feet, max beam: 32.3 m = 105.9 feet). When loaded, the typical container ship looks something like a dangerously overloaded grocery cart. They do come into ports of course. You may have to look close - but there is a ship under there.

Contemporary Container Ship. (photo from www.providence.edu)

Perhaps the best-known mega-ship problem (at least here in North America) is the large oil spill that resulted when the tanker M/V Exxon Valdez ran aground on a reef in Prince William Sound, Alaska in 1989. The tanker was 987 feet long, 166 feet wide and had a cargo capacity of 1.48 million barrels of crude, about 20% of which was actually spilled, causing the single largest environmental mess in this hemisphere to date. The courts found the cause to be:

"The probable cause of the spill was the failure of the third mate to properly maneuver the vessel because of fatigue and excessive workload. Other contributing factors were; 1. the failure of the master to provide a proper navigational watch because of impairment from alcohol. 2. The failure of the Exxon Shipping Company to provide sufficient crew for the Exxon Valdez. 3. the lack of an effective Vessel Traffic Service because of inadequate equipment and manning levels."

Nothing had gone wrong with the ship itself, but it must be conceded that, because of its size, the 20% spill amounted to a lot more damage than would have been the case with a smaller ship.

The best-known, non-tanker, mega-ship disaster is the MV Derbyshire (the British pronunciation is "dar-bee-shire"), a British bulk-carrier that disappeared in a typhoon off the southern coast of Japan with a full load of iron ore from Newfoundland in 1980.

MV Derbyshire (BBC Photo)

The Derbyshire was 964 feet (294 meters) long and 145 feet (44 meters) in the beam and was the last in a series of six identical ships built by the ancient and revered ship building company of Swan Hunter of Tyne. No distress call was broadcast and the 44 people aboard perished. A 1987 investigation declared that the Derbyshire was overcome by "force majeure" during the storm. The relatives of the lost crew protested that "major force of nature" wasn't a good enough explanation and demanded another investigation.

The second investigation determined that the ship probably sank due to flooding of the foredeck through ventilators and air pipes, causing a cascading flooding of adjacent successive cargo holds (It sounds eerily like what happened aboard the Titanic and (maybe) the Fitzgerald too, doesn't it?). When the critical number of cargo holds were flooded the ship apparently dove for the bottom, not allowing time even for a "mayday". The report also made note that standards for cargo hatch covers might need to be looked at – sometime.

But it's hard to see how you could blame it on "bigness". It sounds like it could have happened to any ship which finds itself taking on too much "green" water during a storm that turned out to be worse than expected (and which, from the investigation, could and should have been avoided). If you are taking on water that your pumps can't handle it's only a matter of time, no matter the size of the vessel. Sounds like the first investigation had it about right.

The step that brought the mega-ships to the Great Lakes was taken by the U.S. Congress in the 1960's when they authorized funding to expand the Soo's Poe lock to accommodate bigger lake boats and passed Title XI of Merchant Marine Act, which guaranteed financing and tax deferred benefits funds to build new or modernize existing vessels. Lake Boat companies began building immediately. Along with the government's incitements, they saw operating cost benefits – the labor cost of a 730' lake boat (around 27 crewmembers) is the same for a 1000- footer, but the new ships would carry up to three times the cargo per trip. The first boat designed to take advantage of the enlarged lock, in retrospect, would be a one-of-a kind, transitional vessel. The company that was then called the USS Great Lakes Fleet (US Steel sold it's interest in in the fleet – they are now called "Great Lakes Fleet") began construction in 1968 of the 858' long by 105' wide Roger Blough in Lorain, OH.

The Blough is the largest traditional lakes "fore-and-aft" design, and the last American boat constructed of that design. Although the Stewart J. Cort, the first "1000-footer"on the lakes looks like one, with her fore-and-aft deckhouses, she really isn't – all accommodations for the crew members are in the forward house - the Cort's aft deckhouse is completely taken up by her self-unloading equipment). But the Cort was also destined to be a one-of-a-kind.

The Mega-Ship Era 37

The **Stewart J. Cort**, the first "footer" on the lakes is shown loading Taconite at the Burlington Northern dock in Superior, WS. She was launched in 1972 for the Bethlehem Steel Corperation. (1000 ft. in length, 105 ft. beam. (photo by author)

The next mega ship was also unique. The Presque Isle was the first ITB (Integrated Tugboat & Barge) to sail the lakes. The self-unloading "barge" was built, in sections, on the lakes, in shipyards in Bay City, MI and Erie, Pa. The "tug" was built by Halter Marine in New Orleans, LA, and then sailed around Florida, up the Atlantic coast and down the St. Lawrence seaway.

The **Presque Isle** upbound in the St Marys river approaching the locks in Sault Ste. Marie, MI. The barge+tug is 1000 ft. in length, 104 ft. in beam. She came into service just two months after the Cort in 1972. , becoming the second "footer" and the first SU/TBA on the lakes.(photo by author).

The Blough, the Cort, and the Presque Isle have all been successful boats for their owners but the pattern for the rest of the

1000-footers was set by the next boat launched – Interlake Steamship's James R. Barker.

The James R. Barker (1004 ft. in length, 105 ft. in beam, launched in 1976 to "Plan A") shown upbound at Mission Point on her way to the "head of the lakes". (photo by author)

In all, eleven more 1000-footers would be built over the next six years and, with some subtle differences, they would all look pretty much alike. The Barker is what I will choose to call the "A" design and four were built to this plan, all in Loraine, OH (James R. Barker, Mesabi Miner, George A. Stinson and Paul R. Tregurtha).

The four "A" boats are characterized by: uncovered bridge wings, funnels spaced close together and a high splash rail in the bow. Internally, the "A's" have only two (large) diesel engines driving the twin propellers. The "B plan" boats have a distinctive "T" shape to their deckhouse with the covered bridge wings, widely spaced funnels and a low splash rail in the bow. With the exception of the two USS Great Lakes boats, (the Speer and the Gott), they are all equipped with four (smaller) diesels driving two props with reduction transmissions. The Speer and Gott were also different in conspicuously lacking the traditional self-unloading "boom", as both were initially equipped with the shuttle-type unloader similar to the Cort and Roger Blough. The Speer is unchanged, but the Gott has since been altered with the installation of a 280' centerline conveyor boom.

The seven boats built to the "B" plan, are; Walter J. McCarthy, Oglebay Norton, Edwin H. Gott, Indiana Harbor, Burns Harbor, Edgar B. Speer and Columbia Star. All were built in Sturgeon Bay, WS.

Oglebay Norton (1000 ft. in length, 105 ft. in beam, launched in 1978). She is typical of the "B" design. She is shown loading coal at the Mid-West Energy dock in Superior, WS. (photo by author)

So, here on the Great Lakes, we have built our own superships and they have been running pretty well for decades. Granted, the potential for a disaster is always there, but the environmental issues are not the same. A load of Taconite pellets or coal spilled on the lake bottom is hardly a good thing, but nobody would argue that it is anything like spilling a super tanker full of crude oil. We are focused on ship-watching here; remember that however impressive as the Jahr Viking is, very few people are ever going to get to see her and her mammoth sisters. They are so big that conventional ports can't accommodate them. They just skulk around endlessly from the Persian Gulf to various offshore oil terminals that have been specially built for them. The "1000-footers" of the Great Lakes are available to be seen somewhere on the lakes everyday.

Because of their efficiency, the lake boat companies tend to keep the "footers" busy, and almost all of them are. At mid-summer, 2003, 12 of them are sailing carrying iron ore and Western Coal every day while a good number of their smaller fleet mates are idle. The exception was the George A. Stinson, owned by National Steel. After her launching in 1978 the Stinson had been under charter, first to Interlake Steamship, and then, in the Nineties, to American Steamship. Regardless who was sailing the boat, she ran a dedicated route – loading taconite at Superior, WI, and delivering it to the National Steel plant in River Rouge, MI. Over the winter of 2002-3, National, which had been in Chapter 11, was acquired by U.S. Steel, which didn't decide what to do with her immediately, so she remained in lay-up in Duluth until the fall of 2003, when she went back to work on her traditional route.

The "Thousand- foot Club"

Name	Length	Width	Draft	Capacity (Tons)	Year Built	Owner/Operator
Stewart J. Cort	1,000'	105'	49'	58,000	1972	Intl. Steel Group
Presque Isle	1,000'	104'	56'	57,500	1972	LTV/Great Lakes Flt
James R. Barker	1,004'	105'	50'	63,300	1976	Interlake Steamship
Mesabi Miner	1,004'	105'	50'	63,600	1977	Interlake Stemship
W.J. McCarthy	1,000'	105'	56'	78,850	1977	American Steamship
Oglebay Norton	1,000'	105'	56'	78,850	1978	Oglebay Norton
American Spirit	1,004'	105'	50'	59,700	1978	National/American
Edwin H. Gott	1,004'	105'	52'	74,100	1978	Great Lakes Fleet
Indiana Harbor	1,000'	105'	56'	78,850	1979	American Steamship
Burns Harbor	1,000'	105'	56'	78,500	1979	Intl. Steel Group
Edgar B. Speer	1,004'	105'	56'	73,700	1980	Great Lakes Fleet
Columbia Star	1,000'	105'	56'	78,850	1980	Oglebay Norton
Paul R. Tregurtha	1,014'	105'	56'	68,000	1981	Interlake Steamship

Chapter 7

Alpena (Thunder Bay)

Alpena is a pretty big town as towns go on the "sunrise side" of upper Michigan, with an area population of 20,000. They have a nice mall and an upscale "gaslight" district downtown. Thunder Bay is well known as being a great fishing area and they throw big festivals[1] every summer. The best opportunity for boat watching is to catch a coal delivery at the Louisiana Pacific/DPI power plant near downtown. (416 Ford Avenue (989) 356-8502). It is located on the north side of the Thunder Bay River where it cuts through downtown. The best viewing is from the south side behind the National Guard Armory on 1st Street.

The major lake boat traffic in Alpena is cement carriers serving the huge LaFarge Cement Corp. plant located north of downtown on Rt. 23. LaFarge will not allow visitors onto the gated grounds of the facility, however you can see boats coming and going from the marina park downtown which has a nice boardwalk. (From Rt. 23, turn east on Prentiss Street, then right onto Harbor Blvd to the parking lot) There are basically four boats that load cement and transport it to other cement terminals around the lakes.

Boat	Company	Phone #
J.A.W. Inglehart	Inland Lakes	(989) 358-3313
Paul H. Townsend	Inland Lakes	(989) 358-3314
Alpena	Inland Lakes	(989) 358-3315
Jacklyn M/Integrity	Andrie Inc.	(989) 358-3317

---

[1] Check the events schedule with the Chamber (989) 354-4181.

42   A Guide To Lake Boat Watching In Michigan

These are all cement carriers, a very special type of boat[2]. They also considered some of the most photogenic carriers on the lakes. The three Inland Lakes boats all began life doing something else, however. The Iglehart was built in 1936 as an ocean-going tanker "Pan Armco". The Townsend began her career as a U.S Maritime cargo ship – the "U.S.N.S Hickory Coll" and the Alpena was built at River Rouge, MI for the Pittsburgh (US Steel) fleet and named the "Leon Fraser" and carried ore for many years. All, in time were converted to cement carriers. The Jacklyn M/Integrity is an Integrated Tug/Barge combination of much more recent construction. All are self-unloading cement carriers, which are considered "cool" by boat watchers because the have no unloading booms and thus have the clean lines that traditionalists love. They look like the classic ore boats from the 50's. The phone #s listed above for each boat gets you to a recorded message telling you where the boat currently is, what it is doing, where it expects to go next and when it will get there.

North of Alpena, on the boundary line of Alpena and Presque Isle counties is a quarry called Rockport, which was in past years a busy

Industrial ruins at Rockport (photo by author)

---

[2] They load bulk cement, carry it somewhere and unload it. The issue with cement powder is that it is very bad if some of it gets wet during the process. Cement carriers don't have hatches. They load and unload through shore-mounted pipes which connect to small, circular fittings on the boat's deck and the dry cement is then "pumped" by a combination of mechanical augers and air pressure into or out of the boat.

loading site for limestone. The commercial port shut down back during the Depression, and most of the "quarry" is now overgrown, but you can drive in and see the industrial-age remains of the quarry dock. Be careful walking in the surrounding woods – there are a number of very big "sinkholes" left over from the quarry's operational years. The "harbor" is a popular boat launch site for Salmon and Brown Trout fishing and features a nice picnic area.

Further up the coast in Presque Isle is Stoneport, a busy commercial loading site for limestone. The facility is owned by LaFarge and is located off Grand Lake Road and they see 5-6 boats per week. Call (989) 595-6611 for the scheduled boat traffic. You can drive in (stay on the paved road) and get some good views of lake boats loading limestone. Note: It's a good idea to pull by the office and ask permission - they appreciate that.

Stoneport activity. Two integrated Tug/Barge craft; **Great Lakes Trader** with her tug, Joyce L. Van Enkevort is shown docked at left, and **Mckee Sons** is backing in to the to the opposite side of the dock. (photo by author)

Chapter 8

DeTour Village

DeTour Village

The St Mary's River ends at DeTour, where it empties into Lake Huron. The village itself is on the extreme southeastern point of Michigan's Upper Peninsula on Rt. 134. Boats, upbound or downbound, pass through a channel dividing DeTour on the UP and Drummond Island, about a mile to the east. So DeTour sees virtually all the boat traffic that the Soo sees, except you're not quite as close to the boats. Some cargo is loaded locally from the stone quarry on the southwestern corner of Drummond Inland. A ferry runs from DeTour to the island every 30 minutes.

The ferry landing in the village is adjacent to one of my favorite places to watch lake boats – the Fog Cutter Bar & Grill. This fine establishment is run by a family with long–standing connections to the lakes and the boats, including writing books, a history of the Ford Motor Company's Fleet among them. In nice weather, the Fog Cutter's back deck is a great place to sit and enjoy something cold and wet along with the view of the river – and maybe a boat will come along. If you get hungry, try the whitefish sandwich plate – they <u>know</u> how to do it here.

Walter J. McCarthy downbound at DeTour. The McCarthy is 1000 ft. long, 105 ft. wide and was launched in 1977. She is owned by American Steamship Co. and has spent most of her career hauling coal to Michigan Power Plants. (photo by author)

There is more than just lake boats and the ferry to watch. Salt-water ships board and unload pilots here, and the red pilot boat ties up right in back of the Fog Cutter. The exchange takes place out in the channel and the salties don't slow down. I talked to one of the pilot boat crew who said that it is routine most of the time, but can get "exciting" when there is substantial ice on the river.

Another good boat watching site in the neighborhood is west of DeTour on highway 134. Port Dolomite is a stone quarry located about 16 miles west of DeTour. The quarry is owned by Oglebay Norton, so you can call ahead to check if any boats are expected. (906) 484-2201. You can park in a spacious lot by the office building and get some good stern views if any boats are loading, but don't go beyond the "Don't Go Beyond Here" signs.

RV Tip: DeTour is only 30 minutes from the Soo and less than an hour from St. Ignace if you are staying in either of those places. But a couple of blocks north of the Ferry Dock there is a resort (River Bend Resort ((906) 297-2400) which has tourist cabins and some RV sites (electrical and water). They close after Labor Day.

Chapter 9

Detroit

There exists a rather famous photo depicting a big moment in lake boat history. It is an aerial shot of the Detroit River facing north, with downtown on the left background and a huge ship underway in the middle of the river. The "ship" is the Stewart J. Cort, the first "super lake boat" and she is on her maiden voyage from the shipyard in Erie, Pa where she was built, to Taconite Harbor, Minnesota to load ore. The year is 1972 and residents of the area would notice that the Detroit skyline was different – the Renaissance Center and Joe Louis Arena had not been built yet. Looking close, the Cort was different then too – her bridge wings would not be added for a couple of years.

Detroit's reputation is of a pretty tough town. It takes a lot to impress the citizenry. But looking at the photo years later, you get a feeling that this was an event that people recognized – cars line the Detroit shore of the river and there is a fleet of small boats on the river. A fireboat is spraying a cloud of water to welcome this new triumph of American industry. It was exciting. The thing that we would call the "Arab Oil Boycott" was waiting in the wings along with the Fall of Saigon and…Watergate.

The Cort doesn't really have much history with Detroit. She has never delivered cargo there and has only come back this way a few times in the 70's when she laid up for the winter in Erie. But Detroit has a lot of history with the Lake's shipping industry[1] and she represented a new standard in an industry that had been an important one in the area for over a hundred years. In the 19th and 20th centuries multiple local shipyards built hundreds of lake boats to carry the ore. But the Cort represented something new…and impressive.

---

[1] The Edmond Fitzgerald's destination on her fatal last trip was Zug Island. Gordon Lightfoot only made one mistake when he wrote the lyrics of his immortal piece. The mistake that the Fitz was going to Cleveland probably came from the fact that the Fitz was chartered to Columbia Transportation (now Oglebay Norton), which is headquartered in Cleveland. Her regular route was loading ore at Burlington Northern dock Superior, WS and delivering it to River Rouge.

Detroit 47

The title of this section is a little misleading. What I am talking about here is more accurately described as "Detroit/St. Clair/Sarnia/Port Huron" because that is really the area that is encompassed for boat watchers. Technically, you could include Monroe, MI too, because thousand-footers deliver coal to the Detroit Edison power plant every few weeks. But you can't get much of a view of them unless you have a boat out on Lake Erie and catch them coming or going.

This section <u>could</u> also include Toledo, which is a very significant port and not <u>too</u> far away. I'm personally not picky about it being in Ohio and including it in a book about Michigan, but people who live in Ohio might be. If you are not from either of these states you are probably not familiar with the 19th century "Toledo Strip War". Don't feel too bad if you aren't up on the details, because even non-partisan, certified, Phd-ified, historians are hazy about the details. Allow me to digress a little – this is a pretty good story, but, bear in mind that it <u>is</u> a folk tale. Oh, it happened all right, but there were no embedded CNN crews in attendance to observe and document every detail, so anybody has a right to tell it the way that they want to.

What is not in dispute is that there <u>was</u> a dispute in the early 1800's regarding a portion of land, which would, in the future, contain the present-day port city of Toledo. Sloppy maps and dubious intentions on both sides played a part. After some intense study, here is my take on the affair:

When Michigan applied for statehood in 1833, the boundary between the two states had already been in question since Ohio joined the Union in 1803. The disputed area, known as "The Toledo Strip", had been defined differently by the Northwest Ordinance of 1787 and subsequent federal and state surveys. The official territorial boundary was described as running east from the southern tip of Lake Michigan. Due some pretty fuzzy maps drawn at the at the time of the Northwest Ordinance, it turned out that the southern tip of Lake Michigan was not where it had been previously thought to be. The "new" boundary "gave the "Toledo Strip" to Ohio, who apparently hadn't thought about it previously, assuming that it would belong to Michigan. But when the mistake was made and then corrected in 1818, defining the true boundary, Ohio refused to honor it- they <u>wanted</u> Toledo now.

Things festered at a low level for a while, but in 1833 Michigan applied for statehood and again tried to lay claim to the Toledo Strip. Governor Lucas of Ohio "occupied" the area in question and set up a county government (which is now Lucas County, Ohio). Governor Mason of Michigan (a 19 year old, appointed by Andrew Jackson) sent the Michigan militia south to take procession the "strip" once and for all in 1835.

There very well might have been fighting between the two militias had not the endearing, goofy, incompetence (which seems to pervade this whole affair), asserted itself. Some accounts tell us that the two forces spent a week lost in a swamp near Perrysburg, Ohio, unable to find each other or a way out. What does seem to be documented is that the Michigan militia managed to arrest an Ohio Militiaman, Major Benjamin Stickney (who is characterized as an "Ardent Buckeye" by some Ohio accounts), and hauled him off to jail in Michigan - specific charges unknown. We do know that this insult precipitated the only recorded bloodshed of the war. Enraged, by his father's incarceration, Major Stickney's son, Two Stickney (yes...he had an older brother named "One Stickney") encountered a Michigan Sheriff, Joseph Wood, in a tavern and stabbed him in the leg. It's hard to believe that Quentin Tarantino or The Coen Brothers hasn't made a movie out of this.

Does it end here? No...it actually gets better. The following year in Congress, some very fancy politicking took place, and Michigan, as a condition of statehood, gave up its claim to the Toledo Strip and was compensated with what is now the western two thirds of it's Upper Peninsula. Naturally, Michigan was initially outraged – millions of acres of timber, minerals, hundreds of miles of shore line...in exchange for...Toledo? Well...okay.

Who lost? Obviously, Wisconsin lost. Geographically that land would seem to have belonged to them. But Wisconsin didn't get their act together on statehood until 1848, and lacking voice in Congress, whatever they thought at the time didn't get itself said in the right venue.

Thus ended the "First War Between The States".[2] Everything considered, we would look pretty good to historians if we only could have settled the "Second War Between the States" (which was coming – right around the corner) as well as this one.

Even excluding Monroe and Toledo, this is a big area to cover, but over time, you will find your own favorite viewing points that meet your needs. As with the "Soo", there are a lot of places to observe and photograph lake boats, and also like Sault Ste. Marie, you will find that a VHF Scanner is a real asset.

Way Points in the Detroit Area

As in the St Mary's river, lake boats come under traffic control when they enter the Detroit River (upbound) at the Detroit River Light (about 25 minutes south of Grosse Ile) or Lights 11 & 12 in southern Lake Huron (about 30 minutes north of the Blue Water Bridge which connects Port Huron, Michigan and Sarnia, Ontario). A complete trip through the control area takes about six hours. Traffic is controlled by the Canadian Coast Guard center in Sarnia, Ontario.

Call in Points – Upbound (passage south to north)

> Detroit Light – near mouth of Detroit River in Lake Erie
> Grassy Island (the "Grassy") – Wyandotte, MI
> Belle Isle - Detroit
> St. Clair Crib (the "crib") – buoy in Lake St Clair
> X- 32 (X Ray) – southern mouth of St. Clair river
> Salt Dock – point just south of Marine City, MI in St. Clair river
> Stag Island – Corruna, ON in St Clair river
> Black River – Sarnia, ON in St Clair river
> Lights 1 & 2 – Port Huron, MI

---

[2] Actually...it isn't over at all. We go to war again every November when the University of Michigan and Ohio State University play a football game, ("The Game"), which alternates between Ann Arbor and Columbus. All the fun, laughter and power tail-gating in the world can't disguise the game's deadly serious nature. It's scary to think of what might happen if we lacked this outlet.

50 A Guide To Lake Boat Watching In Michigan

Call in Points – Downbound (passage north to south)
- Lights 11 & 12 – Lake Huron
- Lights 7 & 8 – Lake Huron
- Black River – Sarnia, ON
- Salt Dock – Marine City, MI
- Light 23 – approx _ mile north of southern mouth of St Clair river
- St Clair Crib (the "crib") buoy in Lake St Clair
- Belle Isle (Detroit)
- Grassy Island (the "Grassy") – Wyandotte, MI
- Detroit Light

It is difficult to gauge accurate times between call-in points in this area. You will almost always be off because of all the intangibles. Levels in the rivers change all the time – weather is often as big a factor here as at the soo (more fog in Detroit), and there is certainly more "marine" traffic if you count pleasure boats and salties. The best strategy is to find a place where you feel comfortable and wait – <u>something</u> will show up.

Favorite Sites

I personally have found that the Canadian side of the river(s) offers a lot more access to boats than the U.S. side simply because it is largely undeveloped. Most of the U.S. side of the river is solid with private homes and most of the Canadian side is public land – you can park almost anywhere you want.

Interlake Steamship's **James R. Barker** taking on fuel at Counna, ON. This dock is about a mile south of Sarnia, right on the north – south Parkway. We were parked on the road shoulder.

Detroit 51

That is not to say that there isn't any public access to the river on the US side. Port Huron has an extensive boardwalk, complete with river-side parking, extending from the middle of downtown up to the Thomas Edison Inn just below the Blue Water Bridge (which is a very popular spot). They also have a Museum Ship along the parkway: The USCG Huron, a retired light[3] ship in excellent condition.

Further down the river, Belle Isle, the Detroit public park, is another boat-watcher's favorite. The pilot house of the William Clay Ford is on permanent display of Dossin Great Lakes Museum and has a great view of the Detroit River (It is the sight of the Detroit River Web Cams).

Some of the best close-up viewing is from the "Rouge Bridges". The Rouge River flows east from inland and empties into the Detroit river at Zug Island. Before it gets to the island, it passes through Ford Motor Company's "Rouge Plant", for many years the largest manufacturing facility in the world. Three major streets; Jefferson Avenue, Fort Street and Dix Avenue, cross the river by elevating bridges within the confines of the Rouge reservation connected east-west by Miller street. All of the bridges provide good vantages points for close-up views of boats when they pass through. To get to the immediate area, take I-75 and exit at Schaefer Road.

Interlake Steamship's **Herbert C. Jackson** (690 ft. long, 75 ft, wide, built in 1959, converted to self-unloader in 1975). Shown in the St. Clair River, passing the Power Plant at Port Huron, MI.

---

[3] Light ships were just that – they went out and anchored in a strategic place and turned on their becon light to warn passing craft of a hazard. They might stay out to weeks, even months. They were still in use as late as the 1950's and they often took live animals on board, which were then butchered to feed the crew. Sounds like great duty.

Chapter 10

Escanaba

Escanaba

Like Marquette, Escanaba is a ore-loading port and because it's located on Lake Michigan, it holds records for tonnage – boats can load more because they don't have to negotiate the Soo Locks, and their draft limitations, to reach destinations in the lower lakes.

"The Barker" shown loading taconite at Escanaba. (Photo is by permission of Dick Lund.)

The ore loading dock and facilities here are different than other loading ports. Instead of a "pocket" type structure, which towers over a loading vessel[1], the ore dock here is a shuttle-type, conveyor which

Escanaba 53

moves from one hold to the next. The loader is fed by an under-ground conveyor from the holding area west of the dock . The Taconite comes by train from Pellet Plants located north of Escanaba.

There are no problems getting near the boats for pictures – just drive along the water and climb the embankment. The coal dock (C. Riess) is south of the ore loading dock off Sheridan Avenue. Access is open to either facility. The problem is finding out when a boat is due in. The local paper sometimes prints schedules.

The Kaye E. Barker shown unloading coal at the C. Reiss dock.

The **L. E. Block** is a "retired" Inland Steel ore boat which is used for occasional storage. She is tied up close to downtown Escanaba off Ludington Ave, behind the Sheriff's Station.

RV Tip – After having stayed in the area several times, we again find that the best facilities are run by a Casino. In this case, the Chip-In Island Casino in Harris, which is about ten miles west of Escanaba on Route 2/Route 41. You don't have to go in the casino to use the RV park, which is in back of the Casino – there is a separate office which stays open until 6:00 PM.

---

[1] See "Marquette" section

Chapter 11

Holland

Holland

This is a pretty town of about 40,000 clustered around an inland lake which connects to Lake Michigan. It's history says a lot about the place, the people who built it and their descendents who live there today. Holland was founded, hacked out of the wilderness, by a group of "pilgrims" who left Rotterdam in 1846 for America, just like some other folks had done before them in 1621. And like those earlier "Pilgrims", the party of sixty was seeking to escape religious and economic oppression.

The leader of the party, a minister named Albertus Christiaan Van Raalte, led his flock from New York to Detroit, then continued on alone to find a suitable site for their colony. He found what he was looking for at the mouth of what is now called the Macatawa River where it flows into Macatawa Lake and then out to Lake Michigan.

More than most lake towns in Michigan, Holland has retained the sense of it's of origins. Each spring, upwards of half a million visitors descend on it for a 10-day Tulip Festival. Where you can see people actually walking around in wooden shoes, and, of course, a lot of Tulips. But it was also a "lake-boat" trade town from early on – by 1852 the colony had it's own, community-owned, sailing ship, the A.E. Knickerbocker, to transport goods to and from Chicago.

As a modern-day lake port, Holland, is typical of most – averaging a 50-70 boats per season. Thousand-footers can't get in here; the channel from Lake Michigan is too small.

The dock sites in Holland are all located at the southeast end of the lake.

Verplank Dock – 233 Kollen Park Drive. (616) 494-9499. Various cargos – sand, gravel, stone, etc. This place probably sees more boat traffic than the others. It is adjacent to a nice park (Kollen Park).

Brewers City Dock – 24 Pine Ave, (616) 396-6563, Various cargos – sand, gravel, stone, etc.

James DeYoung Power Plant. – 64 Pine Ave. (616) 355-1243, Coal

Louis Padnos Iron & Metal Co. – 117 W. 7th St. Periodically ships scrap metal to Algoma Steel in Sault Ste. Marie, Ontario. Company does not give out information on schedules.

Other attractions in the general area would have to include the Saugatuck/Douglas area, which is about 15 miles south of Holland on the coast. Saugatuck has a big pleasure-craft marina and several blocks of up-scale restaurants, shops and galleries. Douglas, across the bay, is home to a museum ship, the S.S. Keewatin, a 346 ft wooden-hulled passenger liner built in England in 1907. She is open for tours during the summer months. If you squint, she sort of resembles the Titanic, and is in pretty good shape.

RV Tip: Lake Macatawa Campground 2215 Ottawa Beach Rd., Holland, MI 49424, 616-399-9390

Chapter 12

Manistee

Manistee

Located on Lake Michigan, about 120 miles north of Grand Rapids, Manistee (pop. 8,000+) is a great fishing area and a reasonably busy lake port with 2-3 boats per week on average. If you are visiting, go to the visitor's center (downtown Manistee on Route 31 and 1st Street) and pick up any maps and directions that you need. If you are staying overnight the Manistee Inn gets a lot of recommendations on the Internet from boat watchers. It is located right downtown on the Manistee River where you can't miss a boat coming or going.

A good vantage point for boats arriving or leaving Manistee is anywhere on the River Walk (River Street on the south side of the river downtown. Your best bet is to call the Draw Bridge for information, but they probably won't know anything until the boat is within 2 hours of arrival. First Street beach out on Lake Michigan is a great place to wait for a boat once you know it's coming.

A lot of the boat traffic in and out of Manistee consists of chemicals. There are two fairly large chemical (well, three, if you count Morton Salt.) companies. So you see a lot of Tug/Tanker Barges. One of the rare, real lake tankers, the Captain Ralph Tucker, is a frequent visitor here, hauling brine and calcium from the General Chemical dock. Seng's, which, in addition to being a cargo dock (road salt, slag and stone), is also a pleasure boat marina. Seng's is located on First Street close to downtown and the river, receives.

The majority of the dry cargo coming into Manistee consists of eastern coal for the Tondu Energy Plant located at the south end of Manistee Lake. To get pictures, try the Reitz Park on Main Street. The Park is located on a bluff overlooking the south end of Manistee Lake and the plant. You have an un-obstructed view of the plant's dock, (in fact, you can see just about all of the lake from here) but you will need binoculars and/or a good telephoto lens on you camera.

    Chamber of Commerce – 1 (800) 288-2286

    Draw Bridge – vessel arrivals & departures 1(231) 723-5955

    Martin Marietta Chemicals – 1 (231) 723-2577 – 1800 Eastlake Road

    Tondu Energy – 1 (231) 723-6573 – 700 Mee St, Filer City, MI.

    General Chemica –1 1 (231) 723-6266 – 1501 South Main Street

    Seng's Marina – 1 (231) 723-9444 – 47 Lake Street

    Morton Salt – 1 (231) 723-2561 – 180 6th Street

    City of Milwaukee – Museum Ship 1 (231) 398-0328 - 51 9th Street (but the
Brochure says that the ship is being moved to 111 Arthur St. after October 2003).
Built in 1931, she carried rail cars for the Ann Arbor Railroad System until her retirement in 1981.

RV Tip – The Little River Casino (about two miles north of downtown on Rt. 31) has a brand new RV Park adjacent to it. Full hookups, paved stalls and, a rarity for Michigan RV sites, Cable TV! You don't have to go to the casino, just register as you would anywhere else. The rates were very reasonable - $20/night.

Chapter 13

Marquette

Marquette

As lake ports go, Marquette has been there, and been important, right from the beginning. The first iron ore in the lakes region was discovered in nearby Nagaunee, in 1844 by some surveyors and a year later a mining company formed by one Philo Everett began operations (the name of the company was "Jackson Company" – Philo was from Jackson, MI). Control of the operation would evolve to the Cleveland Cliffs Company, one of the early

Paul R.Tregurtha (see "Queen of the Lakes" in the glossary) unloading western coal for the Wisconsin Energy plant at the LS&I (Lake Superior & Ishpeming Railroad) dock in Marquette's upper harbor. The structure the Tregurtha is unloading into is an elevator conveyor which moves the coal over Lake Shore Blvd (in back of the photographer) to the power plant. It was a "family" gathering – the Lee A. Tregurtha was loading taconite at the same time on the other side of the dock. (photo by author)

giants on the lakes. Cleveland Cliffs, unlike so many other historic companies has not faded away (although they did get out of the lake boat end of the business in the 80's) and they still own the taconite business in Marquette, including the railroad, which brings the pellets up from the plant located near the mines.

Apart from the Lake Boats business, Marquette is a nice college town, home to Northern Michigan University and to some 50,000 residents. There are a lot of things to do in the area, including cross-country and downhill skiing, and, fishing and, of course, snow-mobiling.

The local paper, "The Mining Journal", publishes boat arrivals and departures, but you have to factor in the "Lake Boat Scheduling Rule" – "they can be early, they can be late, but sometimes they will fool you and be on time".

Aside from entering and leaving Marquette, you will see boats docking at two places. The "Lower Harbor" is downtown, and, as you would expect, south of the "Upper Harbor", which we will get to in a moment. If you are coming into town on Rt. 41, the first thing you will notice is a huge railroad/ore dock, which appears to be right in the middle of downtown. As you get closer, you will notice that there aren't any railroad tracks leading to it. This is the "old ore dock" which hasn't been used in years. Apparently, there is some controversy about what to do with it – (demolish or put a resturant on it??). So, for the time being, it just sits there, a wonderful place to hang personal banners "Happy Birthday Elwood!" or "Marry Me, Lavern! (or I'll stop taking my medication and you'll be responsible)".

The "old downtown" ore dock. (photo by auther)

Look south around the curve of the lower harbor and you will see a power plant. This is the "old" power plant, the Marquette Board of Light and Power. Lake boats bring Western Coal from Superior,WI here. As with most power plants you can't get very close but you can get some good views from any place on the lower harbor shore.

You get to the Upper Harbor by going north on Lake Shore Blvd, which winds around past marinas and a Maritime Museum. Like the old ore dock, the LS&I dock can't be missed. The dock is on the "water", or eastern side of Lake Shore Blvd, and the "new" power plant, Wisconsin Energy, is on the west side of the road. I have to confess that this is my personal favorite place for boat-watching on the whole of the lakes.[1] One of the reasons for this is that the LS&I dock and the WE power plant are located in a public park (Presque Isle Park). There are jogging paths running the length of the upper harbor, there are Art Galleries and Railroad Museum exhibits nearby. Not the least of things appreciated here is a free public parking lot about 100 yards south of the dock. You can park and stroll down the water's edge to get great views.

Marquette sees regular visits by 1000-footers, almost always bringing in western coal. The big guys don't load taconite here because the loading chutes on the ore dock are too short to load the holds evenly across the length of the big hull, so to balance the load, a "footer" has to pull out and turn around or move to the other side of the dock. In general, I see more Interlake Steamship boats in Marquette than anything else.

The dock is a fascinating place, especially when two boats are there at once. At the power plant there are huge earth-movers and front-end loaders crawling over a mountain (five or six stories storys high) of coal. Meanwhile, switch-engines are constantly moving railroad cars of taconite back and forth across the bridge over the road along the top of the dock.

RV Tip – The City of Marquette runs a nice RV Park in the woods about a mile from the LS&I dock. Good facilities – nice woodsy atmosphere. 401 E. Fair Avenue (906) 228-0460

---

[1] Excluding repairs and lay-ups, the Lake boats only do three things: load stuff, sail to someplace and unload the stuff. You see them doing all three in Marquette, and you get a chance to really get close here.

Chapter 14

Muskegon

Muskegon

Muskegon is a fairly large (pop. 40,000+) industrial town northwest of Grand Rapids, on Lake Michigan. It is a busy port with boats in and out almost every day, including thousand-footers. Maybe the name of the place is unfortunate – it's a slightly mangled Ottawa Indian word meaning "swamp". It hasn't been a swamp in quite a while, anyway.

The **Paul H. Townsend** unloading cement at the La Farge terminal in Muskegon. The Townsend is self-unloading cement carrier owned by Inland Lakes Management. She is 447 ft. long, 50 ft. in the beam and was built in 1945. (photo by author)

This year brings something new to the lakes – a new high-speed ferry running across Lake Michigan between Milwaukee and Muskegon. The "Lake Express" docks at the Great Lakes Marina, 1920 Lakeshore Drive, off of Rt 31. The Catamaran ferry makes the trip in a little over two hours, weather cooperating, but it cannot carry cars – bikes and motorcycles only.

On a personal note, I became interested in this local because it is home to The Great Lakes Naval Memorial and Museum. The place is located on the south side of the channel that runs between Lake Michigan and Muskegon Lake and it features a WWII patrol class submarine, the USS Silversides and a 30's era Coast Guard cutter, the USCGC McLane. Both vessels are in good shape. Take a self-conducted tour through the sub. If you have the slightest tendency to suffer from claustrophobia (that's me) I guarantee that walking through the Silversides will get you there. Try to imagine spending five or six weeks on a patrol in the hostile waters of the Western Pacific on one of these! Anyway, the museum site is a good place to see lake boats coming in and out of the channel. It's easy to find – there are signs pointing to "USS Silversides" all over town.

In Muskegon, the major operator in the lake boat trade is Verplanks Trucking. Counting their dock at the BC Cobb Power Plant, they maintain four docks on Muskegon Lake. The main number is (231) 894-8265. Try calling them for information on boat schedules. (Pay no attention to the "#,s" – I just made them up to distinguish the different docks.

Verplanks #1 - Mart Dock – 560 Mart Street (close to downtown). There is a WWII vintage LST tied up next to the dock. She is open for tours and reunions during the summer, and is in the process of being re-furbished.

Verplanks #2 Dock – 555 E. Western Ave.

Verplanks #3 Dock – 1920 Lake Shore Drive. This is adjacent to the Sappi Paper mill (address: 2400 Lake Shore), which receives coal for it's own power plant.

Verplanks #4 BC Cobb (Consumers Power Plant) – the plant, at the northeast end of Muskegon lake can be seen from anywhere on the Lake. This is where you will see the footers delivering coal – Indiana Harbor usually makes several visits a year.

The cement carriers come in to the LaFarge dock which is on the other side of the Grand Valley State Univ.- Lake's Research Building from the Mart Dock. (See the Alpena Section for numbers for the Inland Lakes Management boats schedules.)

Muskegon Chamber of Commerce – (231) 722- 3751

RV TIP – Try the Fisherman's Landing Campground - (231) 726-6100 on Ottawa Street off of M-31 just north of the city. It's right on Lake Muskegon. There is also a KOA a couple of miles north on M-31.

Chapter 15

Rogers City (Calcite)

Rogers City (Calcite)

The Bradley[1] sailed from here on her last trip, and so did the Cedarville and large percentages of both crews lived in the area, which has historically supplied a lot of sailors to the Great Lakes, and suffered deeply when they did not return. Rogers City is just north of Calcite, the largest limestone quarry in the world, and so has been an important port on the lakes for a long time.

The name of the quarry, by the way, is the actual name of the substance mined there: *"a mineral, $CaCO_3$, consisting of calcium carbonate crystallized in hexagonal form and including common limestone, chalk, and marble"*. Limestone has many uses, of course, one of which is as "flux stone" used in steel manufacturing.

Oglebay Norton owns the quarry, which is just south of town and can be reached via an access road from U.S. 23. Follow the signs to the visitor's viewing area, which is a fenced parking lot on a hill with a view of Calcite harbor and Lake Huron. The area is large - plenty of room for motor homes/campers.

---

[1] The Carl D. Bradley broke up and sank in northern Lake Michigan during a November storm in 1958. She was on a return trip to Rogers City from Gary, IN where she had unloaded stone. There were two survivors. The Cedarville collided with a salty near the Straits of Mackinac in 1965. Ten of the crew died, nine of them from Rogers City.

Rogers City (Calcite)

Calcite (some of it, anyway) from the public viewing area. You can just see the deckhouse and part of the unloading boom of the Sam Laud behind the piles of stone in the right of the picture. The Laud is an American Steamship boat, (634 ft. long, 68 ft. in beam, built in 1975), and an identical sister ship of the Buffalo (see picture below). (photo by author)

Calcite is a pretty busy place. Usually, at least one boat a day comes in to load, but, as the picture above illustrates, the best views of them are entering and leaving the harbor. Oglebay Norton is nice enough to provide a phone number (989) 734-2117 or 2118 that you can call to get approximate arrival times.

American Steamship's **Buffalo** backing into the loading dock at Calcite. (photo by author)

66 *A Guide To Lake Boat Watching In Michigan*

Calcite gets deliveries too. The **Joseph H. Frantz** unloading Dolomite stone at a pier on the noth side of the harbor. The Frantz is owned by Oglebay Norton and is 618 ft. long, 62 ft. in the beam and was launched in 1925. (photo by author)

Chapter 16

Saginaw River

Saginaw River

The section of the Saginaw River that can be navigated by lake boats runs from the mouth of the river on Lake Huron's Saginaw Bay through Essexville, Bay City, Zilwaukee, Carrollton and then into the city of Saginaw before a lake boat would meet bridges that don't elevate.

Wilfred Sykes (see Special Boats) outbound in the Saginaw River, about to pass the Consumers Energy power plant at the mouth. The Sykes is a regular here on the river with 24 visits in 2002. (photo by author)

The boat traffic is strictly "river boat size". The only 1000-footer to visit here is American Steamship's Walter J. McCarthy, which periodically unloads coal at the Consumers Energy power plant at the mouth of the river – and she couldn't go any further up river if she wanted to.

The boats bring a pretty wide assortment of stuff, everything from road salt to potash. A big general category is called "Construction Aggregates", which includes crushed stone, all sorts of gravel and something called "railroad ballast". And they bring "stuff" to a lot of places on the river. I have counted (so far) no fewer than 17 unloading docks on the river. The stuff is then used locally or hauled someplace else by truck or rail.

The Bay City Times newspaper publishes a section called "Port of Call" everyday during the shipping season. It publishes what boats are expected and lists departures for the week, but the information comes from www.boatnerd.com.

Calumet unloading at Sargent Dock on the Saginaw River in Zilwaukee, MI. Calumet is 603 ft. in length, 60 ft. in the beam and was built in 1929. She is owned by Lower Lakes Towing Ltd, Port Dover, ON and managed by an American subsidiary, Lower Lakes Transportation Company, Williamsville, NY. She was originally a built as the Myron C. Taylor in River Rouge, MI for the Pittsburgh Steamship Company (owned by US Steel, and now the Great Lakes Fleet, Duluth, MN). The photo is a little misleading – the perspective makes the unloading boom look longer than the boat – it isn't. (photo by author).

Saginaw River 69

McKee Sons/Invincible (579 ft. long, 71 ft. wide) transiting the Veterans Bridge in Bay City. This boat was built in 1945 as the USNS Marine Angel and was in salt water until 1953 when she was converted to a self-unloading ore carrier. She was further converted to a barge in 1990 and now works for a U.S. subsidiary of Lower Lakes Towing, Port Dover, ON. She is unusual because, unlike most TBA/barge combinations, the McKee Sons retained her forward pilot house and the vessel is actually piloted from there, manipulating the diesel – powered tug remotely. (photo by author)

Name	City	Phone #
GM Dock	Saginaw	(989) 757-5000
Burrough's Dock	Saginaw	(989) 753-5588
Essexville Sand & Stone	Essexville	
Wirt Stone Dock	Bay City	(989) 684-5777
Wirt Stone Dock	Saginaw	(989) 753-6404
LaFarge Dock	Carollenton	(989) 753-5141
Triple Clean Dock	Essexville	
Bay Aggregates	Bay City	
Buena Vista Dock	Saginaw	
Sargent Dock	Essexville	
Fisher Dock	Essexville	
Valley Asphalt	2981 Carollenton Rd. Saginaw	(989) 754-1002
Bit Map Dock	Bay City	
Sargent Dock	Saginaw	(989) 752-3101
Goderich	Milwaukee	
Saginaw Rock Products	Saginaw	
Dow Chemical Dock	Saginaw	(989) 792-2554

Canadian Transfer upbound in the Saginaw River. This boat is owned by Upper Lakes Group, Toronto, and she is 650 ft. in length, 60 ft. wide and was originally built in 1943. This was originally a U.S. fleet boat, (J.H. Hillman 43-74, Crispin Oglebay 74-95). (photo by author)

Do the boats have to back all the way out to the mouth of the river once they have finished unloading? No, there are several widened sections of the river called "Turning Basins" where they can turn around. One is at the Sixth Street in Bay City, another is located south of Bay City near the airport.

Chapter 17

Sault Ste. Marie, MI (the "Soo")

Sault Ste. Marie, MI (the "Soo")

After exiting the Poe lock the **Columbia Star** (1000 ft. in length, 105 ft. wide, built in 1981 for Oglebay Norton) is shown downbound in the St Mary's river. (photo by author)

Most fans of lake boats would probably admit that this is the most logical place to see them, and the reason is simply volume – most of the boats carrying iron ore (the exceptions load ore in Escanaba, MI) and Western coal have to load in western Lake Superior and are going to carry those cargos to the lower lakes, so they have to pass through here.

A Little History

Sault Ste. Marie is the oldest city in Michigan, dating from the 1660's. The name comes from the French ("Sault" is French for "Rapids"), because that was what the explorers found when they came to the area and there are still rapids here in the middle of the river, between the American Locks and Canadian Locks. The first lock was built by the British and destroyed by the Americans (we were their "Al Qadia" then, remember) during the war of 1812. When copper and iron ore was discovered later (after the territorial issues with Britain were cooled off) there was a period were Portage Avenue in Sault Ste. Marie earned it's name – boats, of various kinds, hauled copper and iron ore from the west, unloaded it on the Superior side of the rapids and hauled the stuff in wagons and wheelbarrows, to points below the rapids, and then loaded other boats for transshipment to the lower lake ports. The wagons were replaced with a railroad, the "Portage Railway", which was an improvement, but somebody always has a "better idea".

In this case, the "better" idea was to move whole ships around the rapids, and this was actually done about fifteen times. Wooden "greased" skidways were built and lake boats carrying ore were actually hauled through Sault Ste. Marie, Michigan towed by oxen. At least 15 boats made the trip before cooler heads prevailed[1], and things got serious about building some locks, which could handle the expanding commerce.

Congress finally approved some funds in 1852 and the first lock was finished in 1855. The State of Michigan ran the U.S. locks until 1881 when the Federal government took over.

---

[1] It took an average of between "six weeks to three months" to haul a boat around the rapids, but this may have been faster than the wheelbarrows.

Sault Ste. Marie, MI (the "Soo") 73

The Locks

Courtney Burton waiting for the MacArthur lock to free up. She is 690 ft. long, 70 ft. wide and was built in 1953 as the Ernest T. Weir. The ground in front of here is a small park located a few blocks east of the locks. The round symbol painted to the left and below the "Oglebay Norton Marine" logo indicates that her bow thruster is located directly below it. (photo by author)

There are five locks in the St. Mary's river at the Soo, four U.S. and one Canadian. Only two of the American locks and the Canadian lock are operating now. On the US side the Sabin lock (built in 1919) is 1350 feet long, 80 feet wide and 23 feet deep has seen no use for years. The Davis lock (built in 1914), which is the same size as the Sabin, is used only occasionally. The Canadian lock is small and is used to accommodate tour boats and other small craft.

The commercial boats, US and Canadian, use the two newer US locks for passage to and from Lake Superior ports. The MacArthur lock was built in 1943 (roughly a year and a half after General Doug bailed out of the Philippines) and is 800 feet long and 80 feet wide, with a depth of 31 feet. The Poe lock was of similar size until the Army Corps of Engineers enlarged it in 1968 to

1200 feet in length, 110 feet wide and 32 feet deep to accommodate the 1000-foot ships. And, no, unfortunately, it is not named after Edgar Allen Poe.[2]

Edwin H. Gott (1004 ft. long, 105 ft. wide, launched in 1979). The "Gott" was built and has sailed for the USS Great Lakes Fleet until October 2003 when the fleet was sold to Canadian National Railway. She is shown upbound in the Poe lock. The lock is nearly filled, and she departed just a few minutes after the picture was taken. To the forefront of the picture is the empty MacArthur Lock. (photo by author)

Long-time boatnerds (that's how they refer to themselves) will tell you right off the bat that ship-watching isn't "what it used to be". Change is constant, but not always welcome by everybody. To put this into perspective, in one day in November, 1943, Duluth, Mn, "...had 39 arrivals and 53 departures, with a minimum of 63 boats in the harbor at any time.."[3]. "During the 1950s and the early 60s, it was not uncommon for more than 50 boats a day to

---

[2] It is named for General Orlando M. Poe of the U.S. Army Corps of Engineers – maybe a relative?

[3] Where the Boats Are, J.A. Baumhofer

Sault Ste. Marie, MI (the "Soo")

pass through the Soo Locks. Now a dozen passages are considered average.[4] So ship watching really is not what it used to be.

Once you get to the soo, where do you go to see boats? Well, upbound or downbound, the boats are on the St Mary's river so just keep going north through downtown and when you get to water, you're there. Actually, you will take the Mackinac Trail (pronounced "Mack-in-naw") north through town and it will dead-end on Portage Avenue at the river. Observe along the way that you crossed a bridge – the downtown of Sault Ste. Marie is an island created by a man-made channel which draws upstream water from the river through an impressive hydro-electrical power-plant on the river front.

And your first impulse, if you haven't been here before, is to go straight to the locks themselves. So make a left (west) on Portage and the locks will be on your right. Now find a place to park – I usually wind up parking in a large open lot about two blocks west on the south side of the street. The reception building is in the middle of fenced-in area with a guard-house at each end of it. The building is open to the public during the summer season, and has numerous displays on the history of the locks. They also post up-and-down bound boat traffic on a board with approximate times of arrival. The gates are always open, whether the building is open and staffed, or not.

You get very close to the boats when they are in the locks, particularly of the MacAurther lock from the elevated viewing stands, but it is not the best place for photographs, because you are *so* close.

West Pier

This is a widely know "secret" among boat watchers, but it appears that it will go away sometime soon– taken over by a condo development. To get there, continue west, past the locks, on Portage and turn off to the right at the gravel drive that runs under the International Bridge.[5] The Pier runs west past the bridge on the south side of the channel into to the locks. You can get terrific views of boats entering a leaving the locks from here, but picture-taking is hindered by a nine-foot chain-link fence.

---

[4] Know Your Ships 2002", Jody Aho

[5] Important note to RV 'ers: turn off to the left and park by the big stone bridge. Do not attempt to go under the <u>railroad</u> bridge just ahead of you – the clearance is only 10 feet.

76   A Guide To Lake Boat Watching In Michigan

Presque Isle (1000 ft. long, 104 ft. in width, launched in 1973) downbound in the St. Mary's river. The small craft beside her is the Ojibway, which, for many years delivered provisions to lake boats (groceries, spare parts – just about anything) The service was owned for years by the USS Great Lakes Fleet, but available to others boats as well. It continues service under new ownership. People who have visited the warehouse (located adjacent to the "Soo Locks Campground) during its operating years compare it favorably to a Wal-Mart.

Mission Point

This is at the far eastern point of Portage Avenue, at the Sugar Island ferry dock. The St Mary's makes its turn to the south here. There is a parking lot and a good Drive-In Restaurant (closed in the winter), but the ferry runs all year round. During the day, it's not unusual to find a dozen or so cars parked facing downstream – waiting to see a lake boat.

The busiest boat on the Lakes, the **Sugar Island Ferry** shown in midstream, crossing the St. Marys River at Mission Point. Her destination, the dock on Sugar Island shows just to the right of her bow. The ferry sounds it's horn each time it leaves a dock.

Sault Ste. Marie, MI (the "Soo") 77

This is an ideal place to take pictures; the angle of approach –upbound or downbound- provides a good perspective of even the big ones. A lot of the photos you see in books or on the internet are taken here. You can see other things here too.

James R. Barker upbound passing Mission Point (photo by author)

In between boats, there are sometimes other things to see: the clock-like trips of the ferry for instance...and the birds. For some reason, the grassy area just to the south of the Drive-In periodically attracts birds. It is not unusual to see dozens of Geese and Sea Gulls scattered in the area. The gulls in the area all seem to be of the same type, but I don't know what that type is. They are pretty big though, maybe averaging about a foot tall when standing.

One afternoon in the summer of 2003 we where parked in our motor home on the edge of the grass, waiting for the Burns Harbor, which had just called in from 9-mile. I was sitting in one of the front seats reading something, when a flock of the gulls descended on the area. I looked up and noticed one gull in particular that had "something" grasped in its beak. – something long and black that appeared to be writhing frantically! The gull was only ten feet from the front of the motor home. I realized what I was seeing – the gull had a live snake, maybe two feet long, in its beak!

I do not like snakes. I realize that I am not alone in this but take no comfort from that. It is a personal feeling and deeply held. If the subject comes up, I immediately picture a golf club. Four or Five Iron. Take a couple of practice swings – don't leave it short. Argumentative conversations on the subject will inevitably include some deluded comment "...but they eat Mosquitoes!" I have never seen a snake eat a Mosquito. I choose not to believe this. Bats – fellow mammals – eat Mosquitos. I support Bats. I provide them with bat homes and nail them up on trees, and that, so far as I am concerned, is that. The outcome is none of my business, but I can choose whom to root for.

Anyway, here is the Gull. He/She is looking right at me through the windshield of my motor home...Gull drops the snake on the ground. Snake tries frantically to escape. No way. Gull plays with snake a little – let it think it could get out of this, then picks the snake up again, tilts head back and swallows. Gull lowers head with tail of snake sticking out of beak and looks back at me...like "Yeah". Then he /she tilts head back again and does sort of an all-body shiver...snake tail disappears. Gull lowers head and meets me eye to eye... shivers all over, like.."damn!!....that's some good snake!!". Yes!! Chalk up another win for the warm-blooded team.

Sugar Island

Quite a few people live on Sugar Island and most of the homes are clustered along the river on the west side of the island. Pick up a map of the island and take the ferry across (they can accommodate Motor Homes). The ride takes a few minutes. Once on the island, make your way to the southern tip (be warned – the paved road runs out after a couple of miles – the rest of the trip is about 12 miles of bad washboard). At the southern tip there is a resort – Lookout Point Resort ((906) 632- 6900). They have cabins to rent and several RV hookups. Relax, you're there. Looking south you see what looks like a lake – it's the Munuscong Channel of the St Marys River. The land mass to your right is Neebish Island and on the left is St Joseph Island (Canada). The only lake boats that you will see here will be upbound – downbound traffic bears to the east of Neebish Island.

Whether you are staying in one of the cabins, or in your motor home, you don't have to keep your eyes on the channel looking for boats – you'll hear them. When a boat enters the channel at it's sourthen end, they sound their whistle – one long blast. Then they come right at you up the length of the channel, and, hopefully, make a turn to the northwest into the Middle Neebish Channel towards Mission Point.

My personal memory of this place is of standing near the resort's fishing boat dock one evening and witnessing an example of what is called "suction" in nautical terms. The 1000 ft. James R. Barker was coming up the channel seemingly right at me. As she made her turn to port, I noticed that the water at the lake edge had receded by some 6 to 8 feet. (I was relieved when it seeped back to where it was before). This phenomenon is called "suction", and it was unknown until mankind built steam-ships of a certain mass. (It was imperfectly understood at the time the Titanic was brought into service). A ten-foot fishing boat with a 6 hp outboard creates the same force, you just don't notice it. The very large propellers needed to move a great ship can produce a considerable negative pressure behind each rotating blade. This constitutes a void which basic physics dictates must be filled somehow. A vessel like the Barker, with 17 foot propellers creates an awesome amount of suction. Small boats which get too close can be "sucked in", becoming part of the "fill", and that constitutes a very bad day.

The Rock Cut

This place is also referred to as the Neebish Island Ferry dock. To get there, take Portage past Mission Point. Watch for a flashing yellow light and veer to the right. This will be Riverside and you will be going south. Take Riverside 13 miles to 15 Mile Road and turn left (east) to the stop sign and turn right on Scenic Drive. Turn left at the sign pointing to Neebish Island Ferry Dock. The river is about a quarter of a mile. The actual Rock Cut is simply a channel just south of the ferry dock, which the Corp of Engineers widened through large rock formation.

Kaye E. Barker downbound approaching the Rock Cut. She is 767 ft. in length, 70 ft. in beam, launched in 1952. as the "Edward B. Green"- name was later changed to "Benson Ford". Interlake acquired her and re-named again in 1989. (photo by author)

Sherman Park

Edwin H. Gott upbound off Sherman Park. She is passing Algoma Central's tanker **Algonova** (400 ft. long, 54 ft. wide, built in 1969. (photo by author)

The opposite of Mission Point and the Rock Cut, Sherman Park is not a busy site for boat watchers. It is a regular old neighborhood on the St Marys River located on the far western edge of Sault Ste. Marie. There is a playground, a sandy beach and a specious paved parking lot with a view of the river. The parking lot is padlocked after Labor Day, but even in the fall and early spring there is plenty of room to park.

To get there take Portage west – past the West Pier and make a right at Esterday, which turns into 4th Ave. Go right at W 4th and left when you get to the river. This road ends at Sherman Park.

River Call-In Points

They actually are referred to as "way", or "check-in" points". Boats, upbound or downbound, are under the control of the U.S. Coast Guard at the Soo, which essentially directs traffic in the St. Marys River.

This is where your Scanner will be of use. After a while the somewhat terse messages you hear will start to make sense to you:

"Soo Traffic, this is the Cason J. Calloway. We are upbound at DeTour Light, draft is 26 feet, 5 inches. Destination is Two Harbors and we are in ballast".

Sault Ste. Marie, MI (the "Soo")

Translation: The Calloway is at one of the way points in the St Mary's River (DeTour, where the river meets Lake Huron), she is coming north (upbound) and is empty of cargo (in ballast). The transmission is routine – under the "rules of the road" at the Soo, every boat must keep Control appraised of their status. Control will answer with a summary of the current water levels in the River and advise the Calloway of any downbound boats that she will encounter on her way north. The Calloway will then acknowledge and sign off, saying that they will again contact Traffic when they reach the next way-point, in this case, the Munuscong Buoy (also referred to as Mud Lake).

The way points on the upbound (below the locks) side are:

DeTour Reef Lighthouse (approx 5 hours from the locks)
Munuscong Junction Buoy (2 hrs, 45 min)
Nine Mile Point (1 hour)
Six Mile Point (40 min)
Mission Point (15 min)
Arrive Locks

On the downbound side of the locks (Lake Superior) the way points are:

Isle Parisienne (2 hrs, 45 min)
Round Island - Light 26 (1 hour)
Point Louise (40 min)
Arrive Locks

Ste. Valley Camp

The Valley Camp is a museum ship located in a large parking lot on the river on Portage between the locks and the power plant. She is a straight-deck ore boat, which sailed for Republic Steel up until 1966. For about five dollars you can board her and take a self-guided tour. It's well worth it. There is also an excellent bookstore right beside her berth selling (in addition to books about the lakes) maps, and other lake boat paraphernalia.

RV Tip - There are two RV parks right on the St. Mary's River. The closest one to the locks is about a mile on Portage Avenue – and it is called the Soo Locks Campground. They will take reservations and try to get you a site right on the river, if available. The second one is called the Aune~Osborn Campground and is also located about a mile further east on Portage. The Aune~Osborn is run by the City and will take a reservation, but won't reserve a specific site. Both campgrounds offer essentially the same view of the river and the boats and cost around $24/night.

Another option is the Kewadin Casino which is about a mile south and has a small adjoining RV park. There are showers and bathrooms, but the hook-ups are electricity only. You don't have to patronize the Casino to camp there and the fee is only $12.00. There are also some RV slots in the main parking lot with electrical hook-ups and you can park there for free for 3 days if you have a Kewadin Club card (which is free – just go to the desk near the casino lobby and ask them to make one. [6]

---

[6] We have done this several times, particularly in the fall and spring, when the casino parking lot is not crowded. We leave during the day to watch boats and shop, then come back at night.

Chapter 18

Tawas Bay

Tawas Bay

This is a special place to me because I live in the area. There are actually two cities on beautiful Tawas Bay; East Tawas and Tawas City. Both are located along U.S. 23 on the bay, which faces south-east into Lake Huron. The dividing line between the two cities is the M-55, which runs inland south of the Huron National Forrest. East Tawas is to the north, and Tawas City south.

The Tawas area has been many things in the past, including being an important commercial fishing port, lumber and railroad terminal (there is a excellent brick Engine Roundhouse dating from early in the last century right on the bay) and lake port. Now tourism (including fishing and snowmobiling) is probably the most important industry, but it *is* still a commercial port for lake boats. About once a week a boat docks at the National Gypsum dock in Tawas City to load gypsum ore. Large Gypsum deposits were discovered just south of Tawas City in what became Alabaster (after the specific white type of gypsum found there) prior to the Civil War. Eventually three companies (U.S. Gypsum, National Gypsum and Michigan Gypsum acquired rights to mine in the area, and continue to this day.

84   A Guide To Lake Boat Watching In Michigan

MV Buffalo loading gypsum (on a very foggy day) at Tawas City, MI. The Buffalo (634 ft. long, 68 ft. wide, built in 1978) is owned by American Steamship, Williamsville, NY. American Steamship evidently has the contract – the only boats I have seen calling here are the Buffalo and the Sam Laud. (photo by author)

"Gypsum's major usefulness to man is its peculiar quality: After being cooked and dehydrated into a fine powder, it can resume its original rock-like consistency by the addition of water plus a few minutes of hardening. It is indispensable to the building industry for wallboard, plaster, sheathing, lath and roof decks, but it has at least a thousand other uses-industrial, agricultural and artistic" (from "Early Times in Iosco" by Neil Thornton).

Today, only National Gypsum is still active shipping by lake boat[1]. To find out when the next boat is due in, call the quarry (989) 362-1844. The loading dock actually has a name, Port Gypsum, although I've never noticed a sign or heard anyone refer to it. But that's what the Army Corps of Engineers calls it. To get

---

[1] US Gypsum still has a mining operation at it's site in Alabaster, MI. Ore from the other operators is shipped via truck.

to the loading dock; go south on U.S. 23 and make a left turn, (towards the bay), onto Lakeview. At the bottom of the hill turn left again on Huron St. for a quarter of a mile and you will enter a gate through the chain-link fence into the National Gypsum loading area – Port Gypsum. There is plenty of room to park and the loading dock is right there in front of you. If you happen to glance to your right, south down the bay you will see a genuinely unique industrial relic – the old U.S. Gypsum loading tramway.

As was earlier alluded to, U.S. Gypsum ceased lake-boat operations in 2000, but it leaves behind the loading system that is a major feature of the bay – it's one of the first things that you notice. "What in the hell is that thing?" is a common reaction. Sometime in the late 1920's US Gyp built a 1.3 mile-long aerial tramway out into the bay, which ends at a loading dock with a large barn-like structure. The system operated like a ski lift moving 72 buckets filled with gypsum out to the loading dock. The purpose, of course, was to avoid repeatedly dredging a clear channel in order to load at a shore-based pier.

As the story goes, one of the supporting towers was dislodged while maintenance was being performed in 1999. This forced the company into a cost-study, which resulted in the realization that they couldn't afford to repair/re-build the loading system and, therefore, would have to scale down or terminate their operation completely.

View of U.S. Gypsum's **abandoned aerial tram** in Tawas Bay. (photo by author)

In addition to boat-watching, Tawas Bay has a lots of other neat stuff – although I'm not going to do the Chamber of Commerce's job here – they don't need me. The town has the busiest Chamber I have ever seen, with something going on practically every weekend year round. East Tawas also has one of the busiest public marinas on the Great Lakes (run by the Park Service).

RV Tip: Just next to the marina is Camping/RV park. Run by the city, it has a large,beautiful frontage on the Bay and full hookups . Make reservations ahead – it's full all summer. (Phone: (989) 362-5562).

Chapter 19

Glossary

Glossary

"Boomer" – Lakes slang for a self-unloading ship (see "Self-Unloader")

City of Registry - Most of the U.S. boats bear the name of the city where they are "Registered" on their stern. Many viewers interpret this as being the boat's home port as is customary with ocean-going ships. Not exactly. Most are registered in Wilmington, Delaware even though most of them could not possibly go there. They are registered there for the same reason that General Motors is a registered Delaware corporation - tax breaks. Canadian ships seem to use the actual city where the company is based. In general, lake boats don't have "home ports". During the winter months they lay up anywhere that dock space is available.

"Footer" – Lakes slang for the 1000 foot length ships built during the 70's and early 80's, following the expansion of the Poe Lock.

Great Lakes "Boats" – Great Lakes <u>Ships</u> - people in the industry call them "boats". This may be a hold-over from when the first self-propelled vessels were deployed on the lakes. They were small and called "steam <u>boats</u>".

"Hogging" – refers to a noticeable, fore and aft convex arching of a vessel's deck, due to unequal stresses while loading or unloading. This is kept within acceptable bounds by skilled manipulation of ballast tanks as cargo holds are loaded. The ambient temperature also plays a part – a properly loaded vessel will hog slightly in hot weather as the deck expands while the lower part of the hull is in cooler water. In extreme instances a vessel

88 *A Guide To Lake Boat Watching In Michigan*

may exceed depth limits and /or serious structural damage can result. A 1000-footer can routinely experience distortions of up to 12 inches. The opposite of hogging, called "sagging", or concave arching of the deck can also be observed during loading and unloading.

MV - Motor Vessel. A boat which is powered by Diesel engine(s), to distinguish her from one which is powered by steam engine(s). The traditional designation for steam ships has been "S.S.", but it seems that Great Lakes boats more often bear the designation "Str".

Marine Diesel Engine – This one happens to be of German manufacture

"New Style Lake Boat" (sometimes spoken with disgust) - Refers to the boat design which began (on the Lakes, anyway) with the launching in 1973 of the MV William R. Roesch (later renamed David Z. Norton) the first "modern" lake boat built with its pilothouse and all accommodations in a single deckhouse mounted on the stern. Nearly all of the boats built since 1970 are of this basic design.

A typical "new style" lake boat, Algoma Central's Algowood (740 ft. in length, 76 ft. beam, built in 1981) shown entering Duluth.. (photo by author)

"Old Style Lake Boat" (often spoken wistfully) - Refers to the ship design which began with the "R.J. Hackett" which was launched in 1869. The Hackett was 211 feet long and 33 feet in the beam. The thing that made her different was that she had two deckhouses, one aft, over the engine and one in the bow for the wheel house. This "fore-and-aft" configuration was unique and it was quickly adopted as a standard - virtually all of the bulk cargo ships that were built on the lakes for a hundred years followed this design - "unique" because nobody anywhere else in the world adopted it. The trend died in the 1970's - the 1000-footer Cort was the last to be built withfore-and-aft deckhouses. Boat fans devoted to the "classic" design often point to a single ship as representing the pinnacle of the classic-lake-ship builder's art - the Ryerson. The Edward L. Ryerson was launched in 1960 as a steam-powered, non self-unloader (see "Straight-Decker"). She was nearly obsolete when her stem hit the water – but with her sleek, artdeco lines, she was pretty to look at, and reportedly very fast "running up and down the lake". But taking over 24 hours to unload cargo wasn't competitive - and she now is laid up in Sturgeon Bay, WI. and may never come back to work. Another nice example is the Reserve built in 1953 (see below). She was converted to a self-unloader and is still steaming every day.

Str. Reserve (767 ft. in length, 70 ft. beam, launched in 1952) shown downbound at the Rock Cut, St Mary's River.(photo by author)

Queen of the Lakes – A traditional honorary title awarded to the current biggest boat in operation on the lakes. This title has changed hands many times, and has been held by such well-known ships as the Cliffs Victory (March 3, 1957 to June, 7, 1958) and the Edmund Fitzgerald (June7, 1958 to January 26, 1960). The current "Queen" is Interlake Steamship's Paul R. Tregurtha, which is listed officially as being 1013 ft. 6 in. She has held the title since April 25, 1981, which just beats the record of 22 years held by the Carl D. Bradley – 1927 to 1949. The Tregurtha is not the most powerful boat on the lakes, however. That honor belongs to the USS Great Lakes Fleet's Edwin H.Gott, which can call up 19,500 hp from it's twin diesels (the Tregurtha's diesels are rated at 17,129 hp). The Speer is not the fastest ore carrier, though. That honor belongs to the Cort which is rated at 18.4 mph. (the Speer can only manage 16.7 and the Tregurtha 15.5). Maybe we should put all this in perspective though - the British battleship HMS Hood, built in 1918, was rated at 144,000 hp.

MV Paul R. Treguertha. (1014 ft. in length, 105 ft. in beam, launched in 1981) shown downbound in the St. Mary's River. (photo by author)

Salty – Great Lakes slang for an ocean-going ship. Salty's enter the lakes through the St. Lawrence and the Welland Canal.

Self-Unloader - The term "self-unloader" in relation to a Great Lakes ship means simply that the ship is equipped to do just that - unload its bulk cargo onto an adjacent pier. This technology was developed early in the 20th century and it revolutionized the Great Lakes shipping industry. Self-unloaders utilize a fundamental principal -gravity. A self-unloader's cargo holds are shaped like giant funnels inside the ship's hull. When unloading bulk cargo, iron (Taconite) pellets for example, a hatch is opened at the bottom of a selected hold and the pellets drop onto a conveyer, which runs the length of the ship beneath the holds. This conveyor transports the cargo up to a hopper, which feeds the cargo out onto the pier via the unloading boom conveyor- usually about 250 feet in length. This technology was developed on the

Self-Unloader **Agawa Canyon** unloads stone on the Saginaw River. She is 647 ft. in length, 72 ft. in the beam and was built in 1970. She is owned by Algoma Central, Sault Ste. Marie, ON)

lakes and remains very nearly unique to the lakes. The first lake boat to be built as a self-unloader was the Str. Wyandotte in 1908

Straight-decker **Cedarglen** She is 730 ft. long, 75 ft. wide and was built in Germany in 1959. She is owned by Canada Steamship Lines. (photo by author)

at Great Lakes Engineering in Ecorse, MI and her active career lasted until 1966.

Side Thruster – A propeller mounted at a right-angle to the boats keel. Allows boat to move sideways when alongside a pier. Often mounted in both bow and stern.

Straight-decker – Lake's slang for a boat that lacks self-unloading capability. Currently, none are active in the U.S. fleet. The last U.S. straight-decker to work the lakes, the Kinsmen Independent, was retired in December, 2002. The Canadian fleet maintains a number of "straight-deckers" however. Non-Self-Unloading ships are also commonly referred to as "Bulk Carriers".

Taconite – In geological terms, Taconite is a type of rock containing iron ore in about a 25% concentration. When veins of purer ore began to become scarce in the 1950's, scientist's at the University of Minnesota developed a process for extracting the iron from the Taconite rock. After being blasted into small pieces as it is mined, the rock is transported to mills which crush and separate the iron from the waste rock using magnets. The iron is then processed into marble-sized "Taconite" pellets. Taconite constitutes the largest single

TBA Joyce L. Van Enkevort (tug)/Great Lakes Trader(barge) in the Saginaw River (photo by author)

commodity for the Great Lakes shipping industry.

TBA – Articulated Tug/Barge (also referred to as "ITB - Integrated Tug/Barge"). A specially designed tug boat which fits into a "pocket" in the stern of a barge, which mounts a self-unloading system. The resulting combination looks like a standard lake boat. The connection is accomplished by links and hydraulic pads on the tug's bow. This is a fairly recent innovation on the lakes - the first was the 1000-footer Presque Isle. For more information on TBA's see: www.oceantugbarge.com/

Appendix A. U.S. and Canadian Fleets as of October, 2003

Note: these tables list only commercial cargo carriers. Tugboats and other auxilliary vessels are excluded.

U.S. FLEET Key to Type: BC = Bulk Carrier CC = Cement Carrier GC = General SU = Self-Unloader

Ship Name	Type	Company	Capacity(tons)	Length (ft)	Year Built	Age
1 Adam E. Cornelius	SU	American Steamship	28,200	680	1973	30
2 American Mariner	SU	American Steamship	37,200	730	1980	23
3 American Republic	SU	American Steamship	24,800	634	1981	22
4 Buffalo	SU	American Steamship	23,800	634	1978	25
5 H.Lee White	SU	American Steamship	35,200	704	1974	29
6 Indiana Harbor	SU	American Steamship	78,850	1000	1979	24
7 John J Boland	SU	American Steamship	33,800	680	1973	30
8 Sam Laud	SU	American Steamship	23,800	634	1975	28
9 St.Clair	SU	American Steamship	44,000	770	1976	27
10 George A. Stinson*	SU	American Steamship	59,700	1004	1978	25
11 Walter J. McCarthy	SU	American Steamship	78,850	1000	1977	26
12 Burns Harbor	SU	International Steel Group	78,850	1000	1980	23
13 Stewart J. Cort	SU	International Steel Group	58,000	1000	1972	31
14 Edward L.Ryerson*	BC	Central Marine Logistics	27,500	730	1960	43
15 Joseph L. Block	SU	Central Marine Logistics	37,200	728	1976	27
16 Wilfred Sykes	SU	Central Marine Logistics	21,500	678	1949	54
17 Kinsmen Independent*	BC	Great Lakes Associates	18,800	642	1952	51
18 Arthur M. Anderson*	SU	Great Lakes Fleet	25,300	767	1952	51
19 Cason J. Callaway*	SU	Great Lakes Fleet	25,300	767	1952	51

Appendix 95

20 Edgar B. Speer*	SU	Great Lakes Fleet	73,700	1004	1980	23
21 Edwin H. Gott*	SU	Great Lakes Fleet	74,100	1004	1979	24
22 John J. Munson*	SU	Great Lakes Fleet	25,500	768	1952	51
23 Philip R. Clark*	SU	Great Lakes Fleet	25,300	767	1952	51
24 Roger Blough*	SU	Great Lakes Fleet	43,900	858	1972	31
25 Presque Isle*	SU/TBA	Great Lakes Fleet	57,500	1000	1973	30
26 Alpena	CC	Inland Lakes Mgt.	15,500	519	1942	61
27 E.M.Ford	CC	Inland Lakes Mgt.	7,100	428	1898	105
28 J.A.W. Iglehart	CC	Inland Lakes Mgt.	12,500	501	1936	67
29 Paul H. Townsend	CC	Inland Lakes Mgt.	8,400	447	1945	58
30 S.T. Crapo	CC	Inland Lakes Mgt.	8,900	402	1927	76
31 Charles M. Beeghly	SU	Interlake Steamship	31,000	806	1959	44
32 Elton Hoyt 2nd*	SU	Interlake Steamship	22,300	698	1952	51
33 Herbert C. Jackson	SU	Interlake Steamship	24,800	690	1959	44
34 James R. Barker	SU	Interlake Steamship	63,300	1004	1976	27
35 Mesabi Miner	SU	Interlake Steamship	63,300	1004	1977	26
36 Paul R. Tregurtha	SU	Interlake Steamship	68,000	1014	1981	22
37 Pathfinder	SU/TBA	Interlake Steamship	21,260	700	2001	2
38 Lee A. Tregurtha	SU	Interlake Steamship	29,300	826	1942	61
39 Kaye E. Barker	SU	Interlake Steamship	25,900	767	1952	51
40 John Sherwin	BC	Interlake Steamship	31,500	806	1958	45
41 Armco	SU	Oglebay Norton	25,500	767	1953	50
42 Buckeye	SU	Oglebay Norton	22,300	698	1952	51
43 Columbia Star	SU	Oglebay Norton	78,850	1000	1978	25
44 Courtney Burton	SU	Oglebay Norton	22,300	690	1953	50

#	Name	Type	Owner	Capacity	Year	Age
45	David Z. Norton	SU	Oglebay Norton	19,650	1973	30
46	Earl W. Oglebay	SU	Oglebay Norton	19,650	1973	30
47	Fred R. White	SU	Oglebay Norton	23,800	1979	24
48	Joseph H. Frantz	SU	Oglebay Norton	13,600	1925	78
49	Middletown	SU	Oglebay Norton	26,300	1942	61
50	Oglebay Norton	SU	Oglebay Norton	78,850	1978	25
51	Reserve	SU	Oglebay Norton	25,500	1953	50
52	Wolverine	SU	Oglebay Norton	19,650	1974	29
53	Southdown Challenger	CC	HMC Ship Management	16300	1906	98
54	Southdown Conquest	CC	HMC Ship Management	8500	1937	67
53	Joseph H. Thompson/JR	SU/TBA	Upper Lakes Towing	21,200	1990	13
54	Great Lakes Trader	SU/TBA	Van Enkevort Tug & Barge	39,600	2000	3

Total U.S. Fleet Capicity (tons)   1,955,260   Avg.Age: 40.25

Notes:
George A. Stinson   Owned by National Steel - chartered to American Steamship. National acquired by U.S. Steel in 2003. Laid up in Duluth for most of 2003 season, re-named "American Spirit""

Edward L. Ryerson   Laid up in Sturgen Bay, WS since 1998.
Kinsmen Independent   Retired in Buffalo - status undetermined

Great Lakes Fleet   CN (Canadian National railway) acquired parent co. in Oct, 2003, fully operational

Elton Hoyt 2nd   Sold to Lower Lakes Towing (Canada) - and renamed Michipicoten in 2003

Appendix 97

CANADIAN FLEET Key to Type: BC = Bulk Carrier CC = Cement Carrier GC = General SU = Self-Unloader

Ship Name	Type	Company	Capacity(tons)	Length (ft)	Year Built	Age
1 Agawa Canyon	SU	Algoma Central	23,400	647	1970	33
2 Algobay	SU	Algoma Central	34,900	730	1978	25
3 Algocape	BC	Algoma Central	29,950	729	1967	36
4 Algocen	BC	Algoma Central	28,400	730	1968	35
5 Algoisle	BC	Algoma Central	26,700	730	1963	40
6 Algolake	SU	Algoma Central	32,150	730	1977	26
7 Algomarine	SU	Algoma Central	27,000	729	1968	35
8 Algonorth	BC	Algoma Central	28,000	729	1971	32
9 Algontario	BC	Algoma Central	29,100	730	1960	43
10 Algoport	SU	Algoma Central	32,000	658	1979	24
11 Algorail	SU	Algoma Central	23,750	640	1968	35
12 Algosoo	SU	Algoma Central	31,300	730	1974	29
13 Algosound	BC	Algoma Central	27,700	730	1965	38
14 Algosteel	SU	Algoma Central	27,000	729	1966	37
15 Algoville	SU	Algoma Central	31,250	730	1967	36
16 Algoway	SU	Algoma Central	24,000	650	1972	31
17 Algowood	SU	Algoma Central	31,750	740	1981	22
18 Capt.Henry Jackman	SU	Algoma Central	30,550	730	1981	22
19 John B.Aird	SU	Algoma Central	31,300	730	1983	20
20 Peter R. Cresswell	SU	Algoma Central	31,700	730	1982	21
21 Sauniere	SU	Societe Quebecois	23,900	642	1970	33
22 Alantic Erie	SU	Canada Steamship	38,200	736	1985	18

98 A Guide To Lake Boat Watching In Michigan

23	Alantic Huron	SU	Canada Steamship	34,600	736	1984	19
24	Birchglen	BC	Canada Steamship	35,315	730	1983	20
25	Cedarglen	BC	Canada Steamship	29,100	730	1959	44
26	CSL Laurentien	SU	Canada Steamship	34,938	739	1977	26
27	CSL Niagara	SU	Canada Steamship	34,938	739	1972	31
28	CSL Tadoussac	SU	Canada Steamship	29,700"	730	1969	34
29	Ferbec	BC	Canada Steamship	56,887	732	1966	37
30	Frontenac	SU	Canada Steamship	27,500	729	1968	35
31	Halifax	SU	Canada Steamship	30,100	730	1963	40
32	Jean Parisien	SU	Canada Steamship	33,000	730	1977	26
33	Mapleglen	BC	Canada Steamship	26,100	714	1960	43
34	Nanticoke	SU	Canada Steamship	35,100	729	1980	23
35	Oakglen	BC	Canada Steamship	22,950	714	1954	49
36	Pineglen	BC	Canada Steamship	32,600	736	1985	18
37	Rt.Hon.Paul J.Martin	SU	Canada Steamship	34,938	739	1973	30
38	Spruceglen	BC	Canada Steamship	35,315	730	1983	20
39	Teakglen	BC	Canada Steamship	17,650	607	1967	36
40	English River	CC	Canada Steamship	7,450	404	1961	42
41	Betsiamites	SU	Le Groupe Ocean	11,600	402	1969	34
42	Cuyahoga	SU	Lower Lakes Towing	15,675	620	1943	60
43	Mississagi	SU	Lower Lakes Towing	15,800	620	1943	60
44	Saginaw	SU	Lower Lakes Towing	20,200	639	1953	50
45	Calumet	SU	Lower Lakes Towing	12,450	603	1929	74
46	Maumee	SU	Lower Lakes Towing	12,650	604	1929	74
47	McKee Sons	SU/TBA	Lower Lakes Towing	19,900	604	1945	58

48 Gordon C. Leitch	BC	Upper Lakes Group	29,700	730	1968	35
49 Canadian Enterprise	SU	Upper Lakes Group	35,100	730	1979	24
50 Canadian Leader	BC	Upper Lakes Group	28,300	730	1967	36
51 Canadian Mariner	BC	Upper Lakes Group	27,700	730	1963	40
52 Canadian Miner	BC	Upper Lakes Group	28,050	730	1966	37
53 Canadian Navigator	SU	Upper Lakes Group	30,925	728	1967	36
54 Canadian Olympic	SU	Upper Lakes Group	35,100	730	1976	27
55 Canadian Progress	SU	Upper Lakes Group	32,700	730	1968	35
56 Canadian Prospector	BC	Upper Lakes Group	30,500	730	1964	39
57 Canadian Transfer	SU	Upper Lakes Group	27,450	650	1943	60
58 Canadian Transport	SU	Upper Lakes Group	25,900	730	1979	24
59 James Norris	SU	Upper Lakes Group	35,100	663	1952	51
60 John D. Leitch	SU	Upper Lakes Group	31,600	730	1967	36
61 Montrealais	BC	Upper Lakes Group	27,800	730	1962	41
62 Quebecois	BC	Upper Lakes Group	27,800	730	1963	40
63 Seaway Queen	BC	Upper Lakes Group	24,300	713	1959	44
64 Amelia Desgagnes	GC	Group Desgagnes	7,126	355	1976	27
65 Catherine Desgagnes	GC	Group Desgagnes	8,350	410	1962	41
66 Cecelia Desgagnes	GC	Group Desgagnes	7,875	374	1971	32
67 Jacques Desgagnes	GC	Group Desgagnes	1,250	208	1960	43
68 Mathilda Desgagnes	GC	Group Desgagnes	6,920	360	1950	53
69 Melissa Desgagnes	GC	Group Desgagnes	7,000	355	1975	28

Total Canadian Fleet Capacity (tons)- 1,827,002.00   Avg.Age   35.99